STUDIES FOR THE OTHER ART FAIR

NOVEMBER 2017

32 PAINTINGS
8 x 8 x .75 inches
oil paint, cold wax medium & marble dust on canvas

stephen cimini

ARTIST CONTACT
stephencimini@gmail.com
www.stephencimini.com

Copyright © 2017 stephen cimini
All rights reserved. No part of this publication may be reproduced in any form without the written permission of the author.

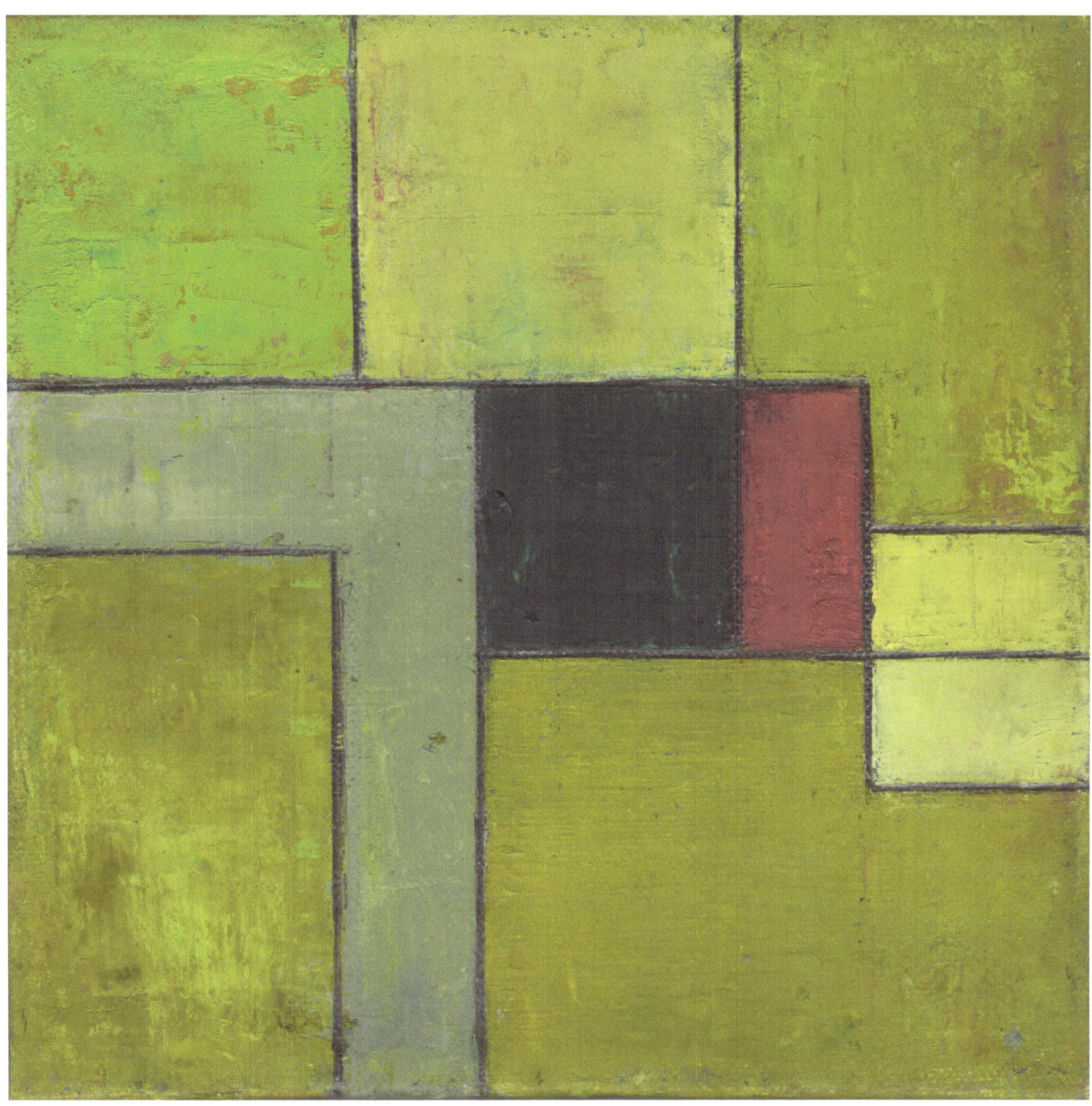

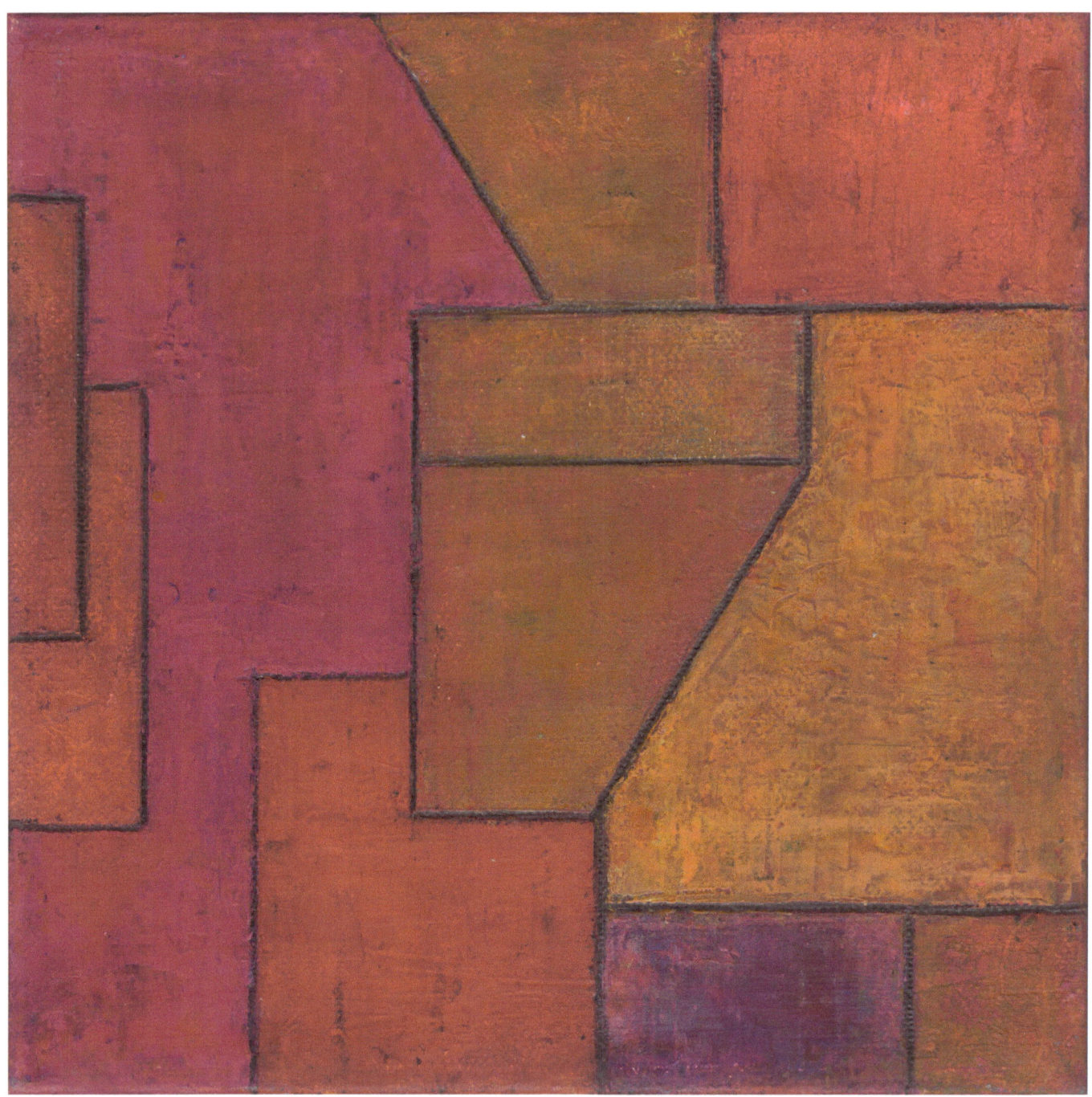

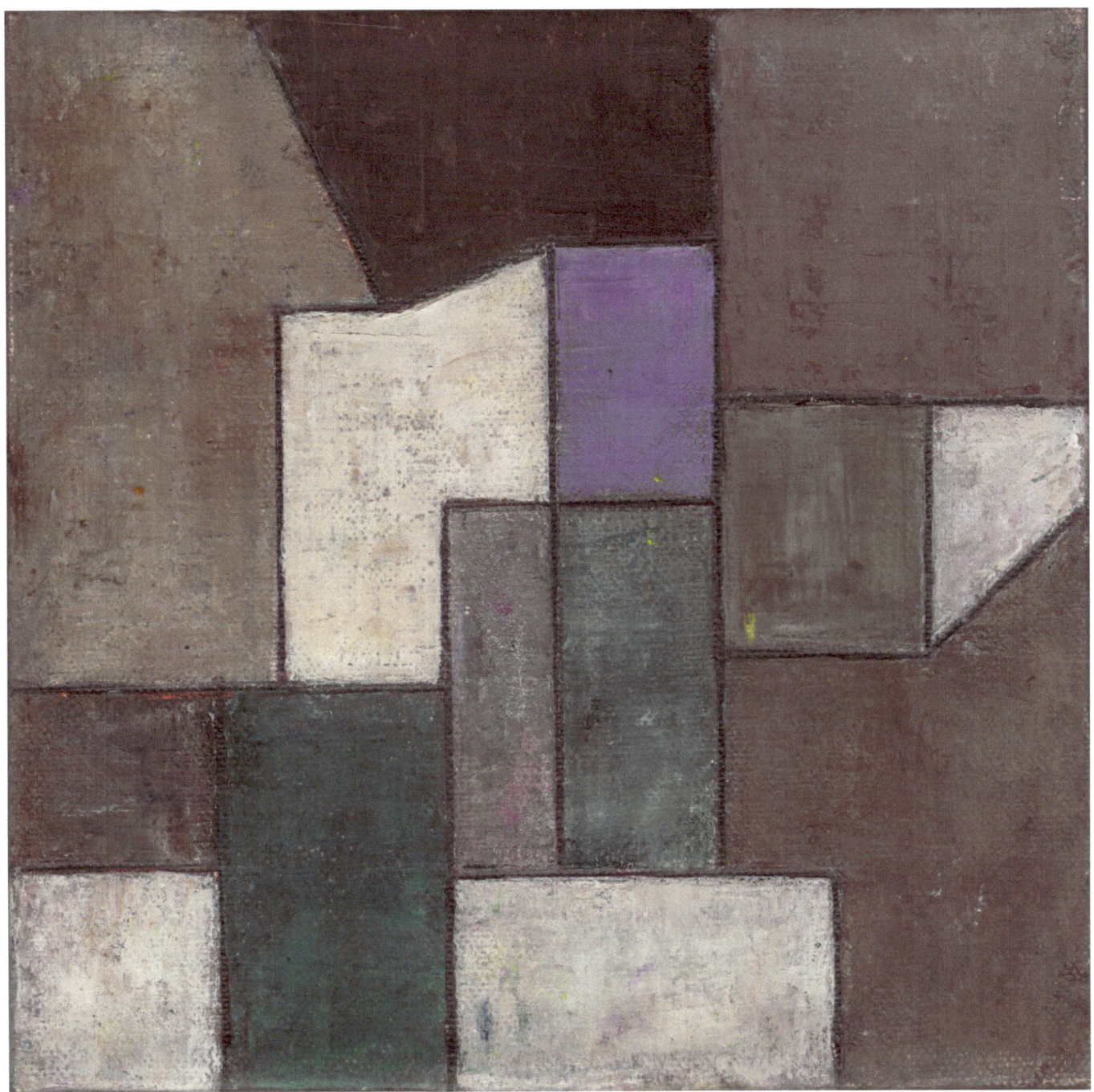

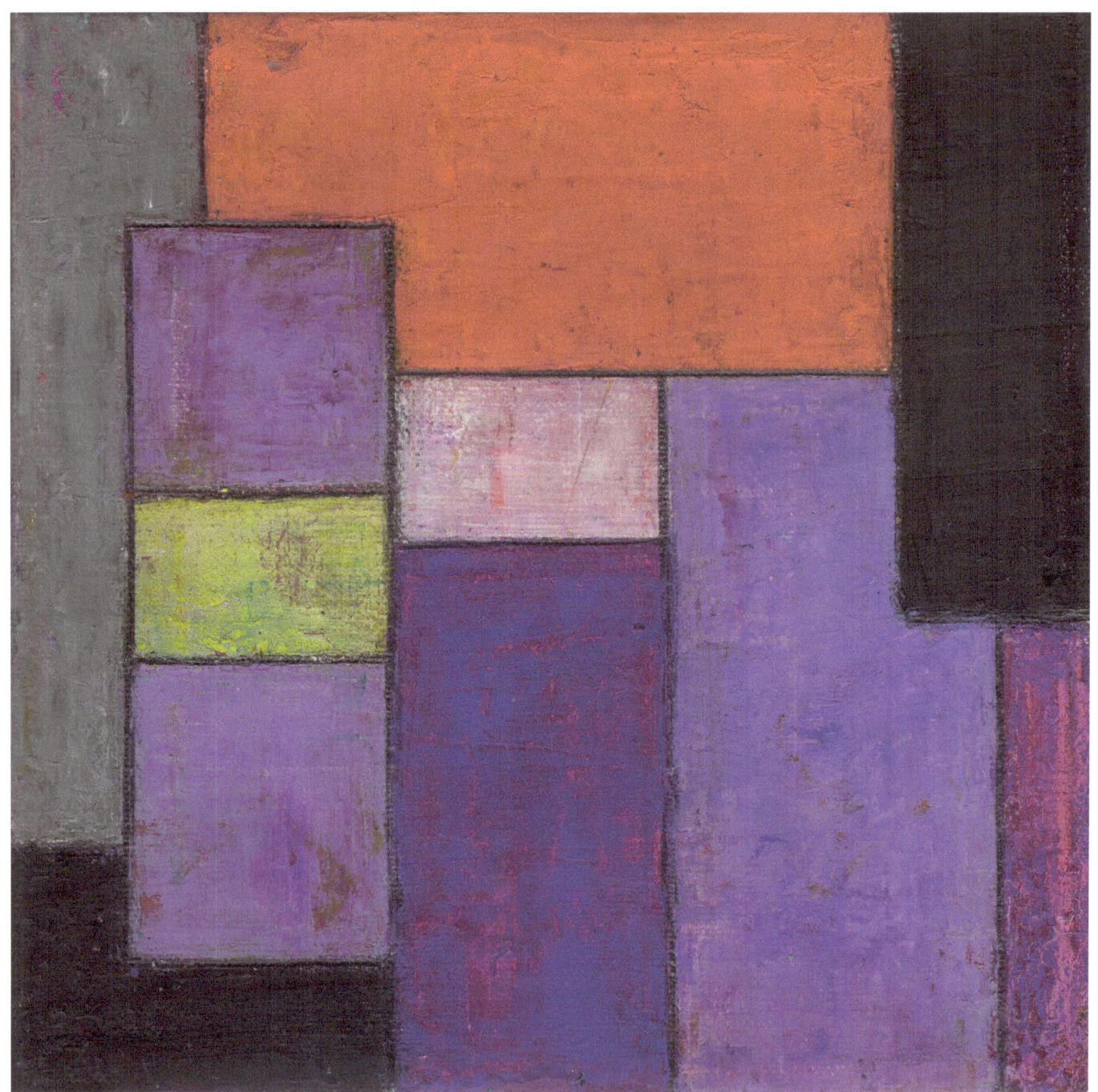

4

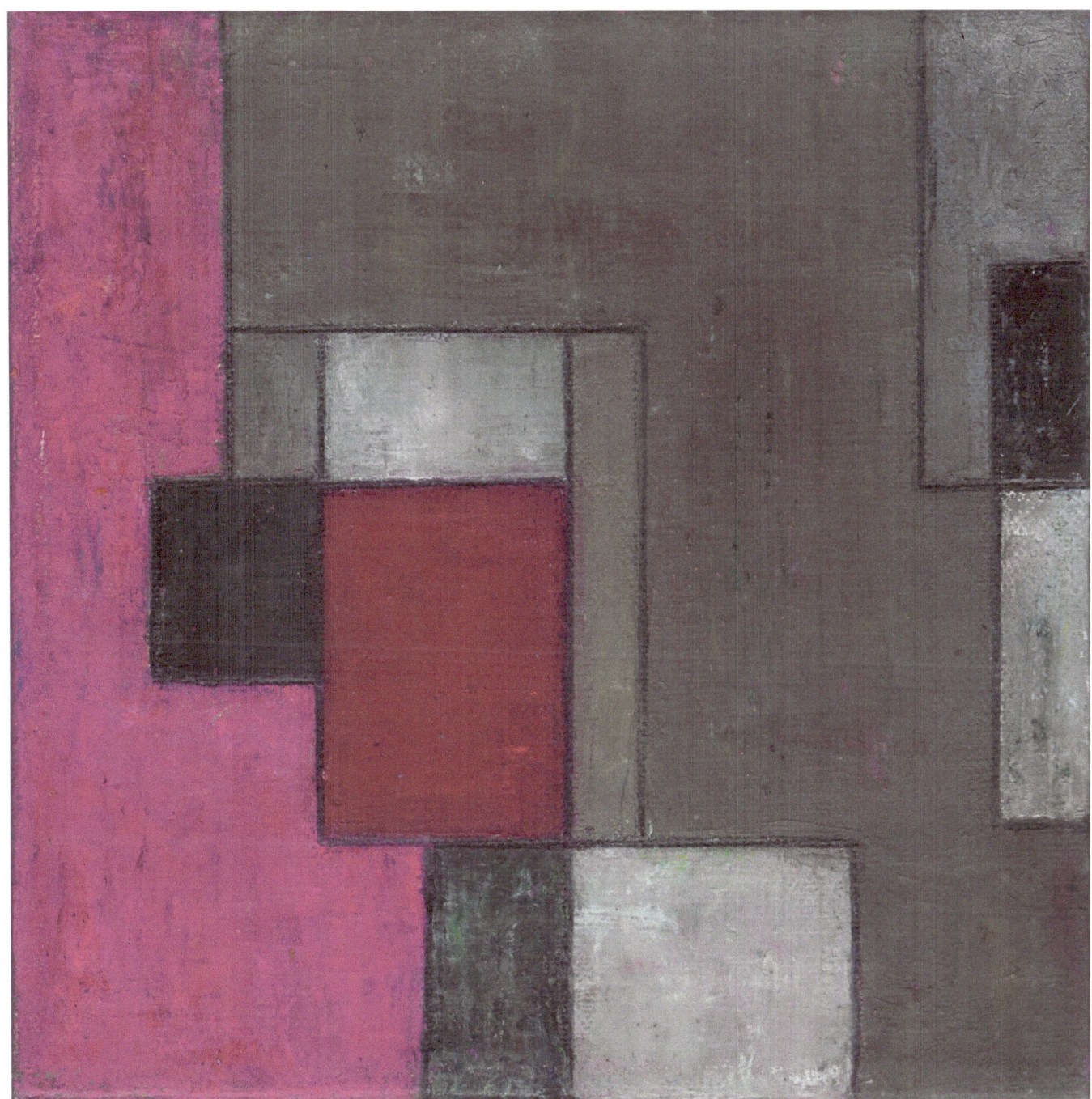

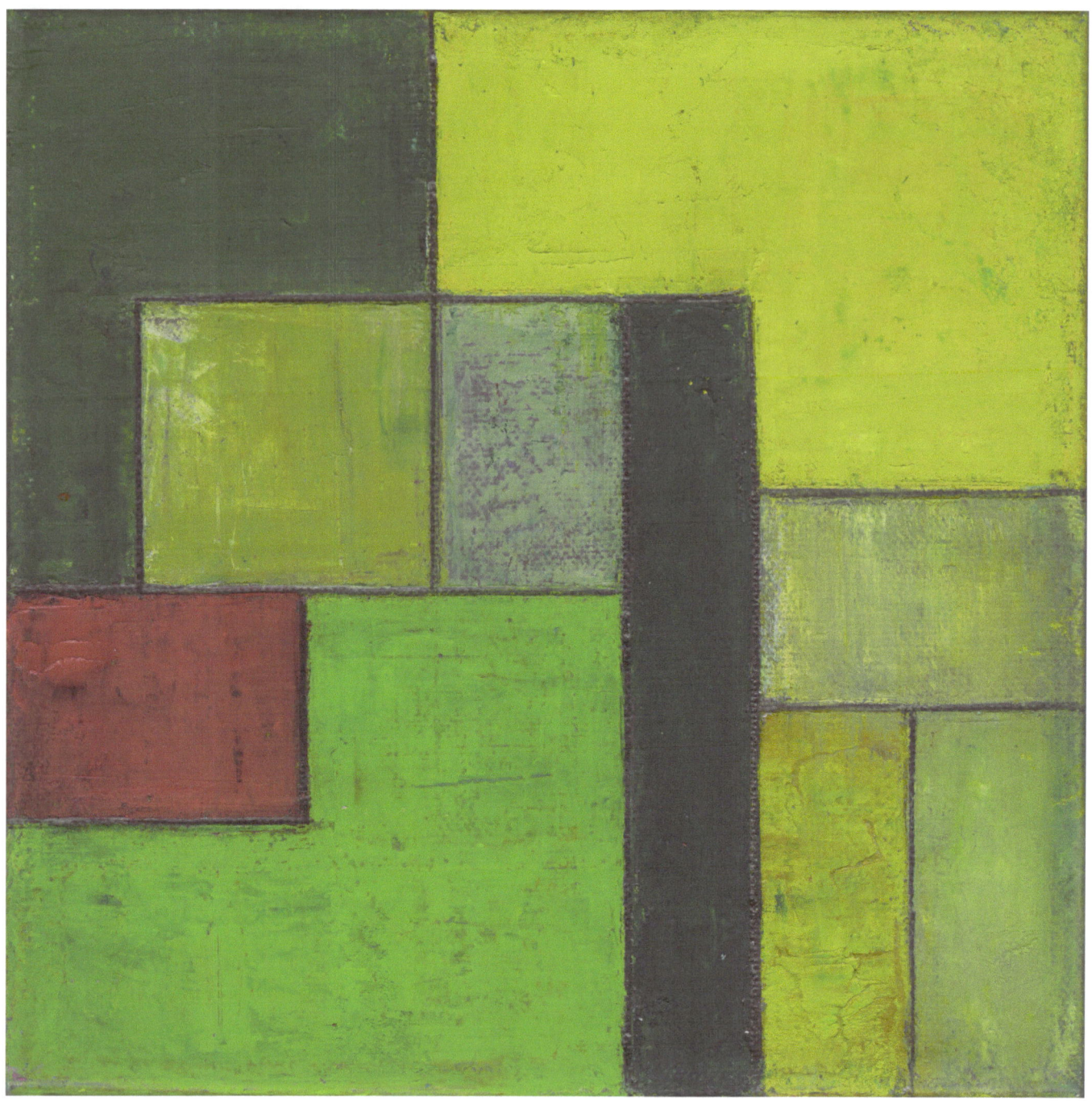

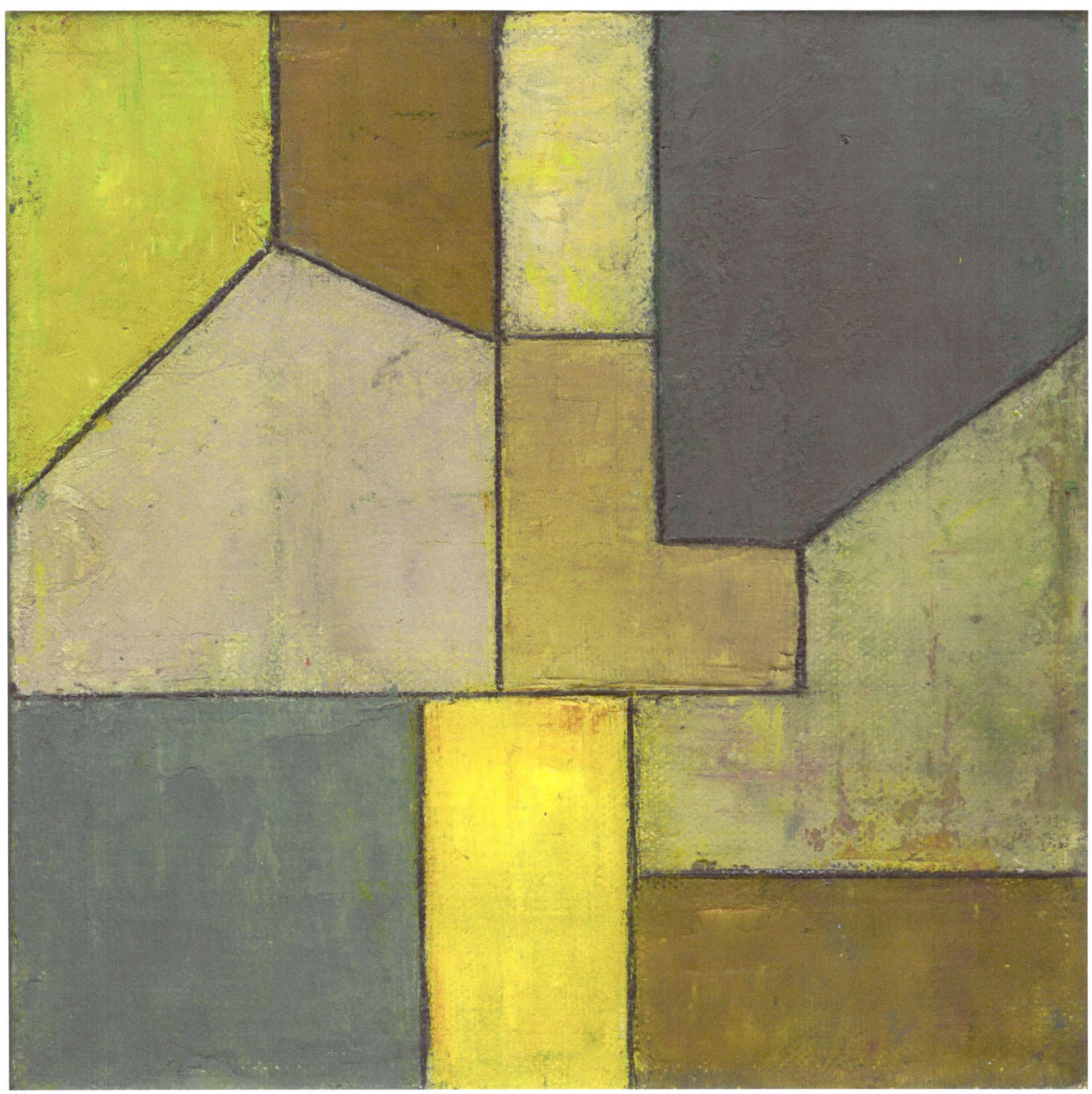

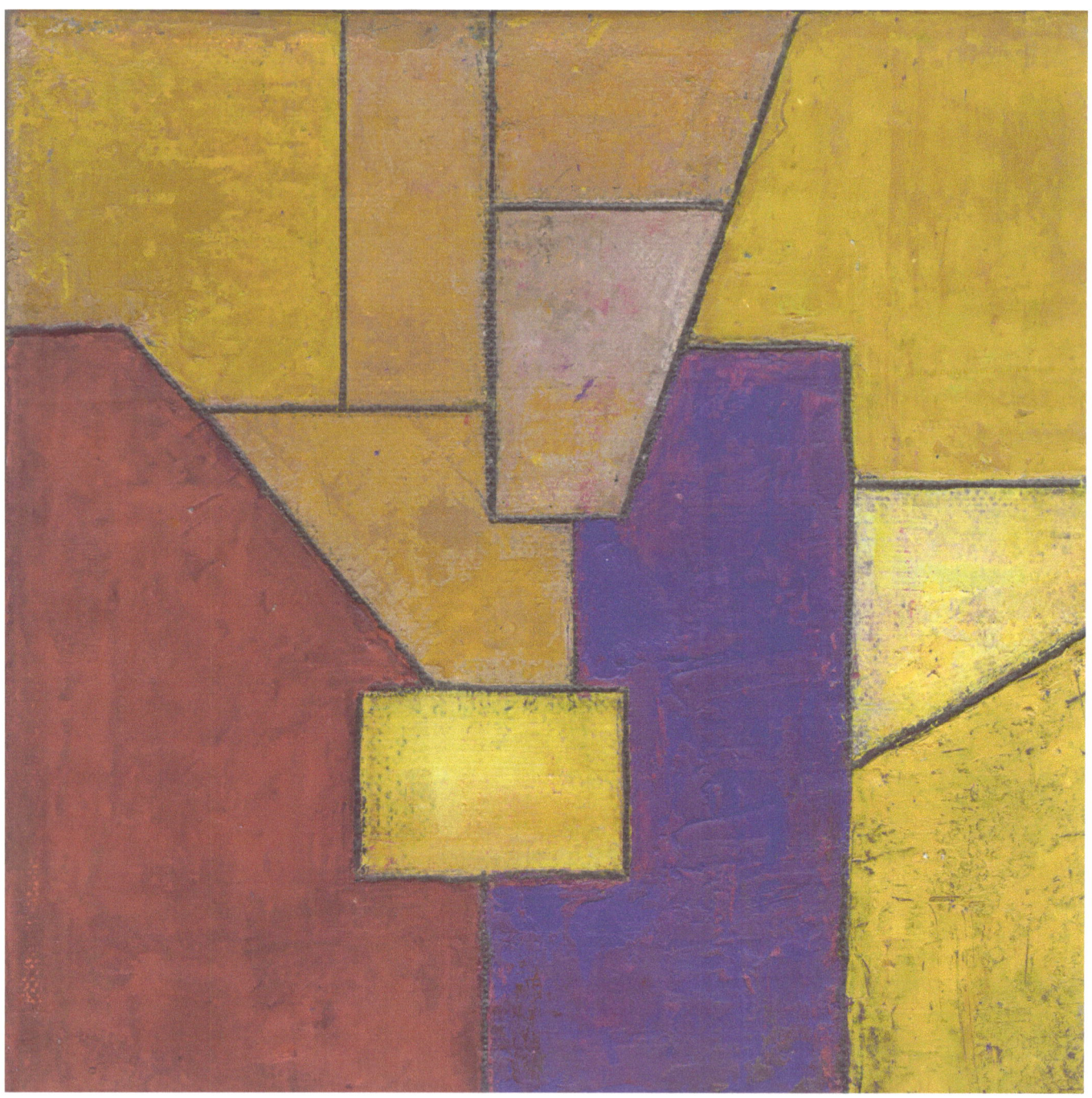

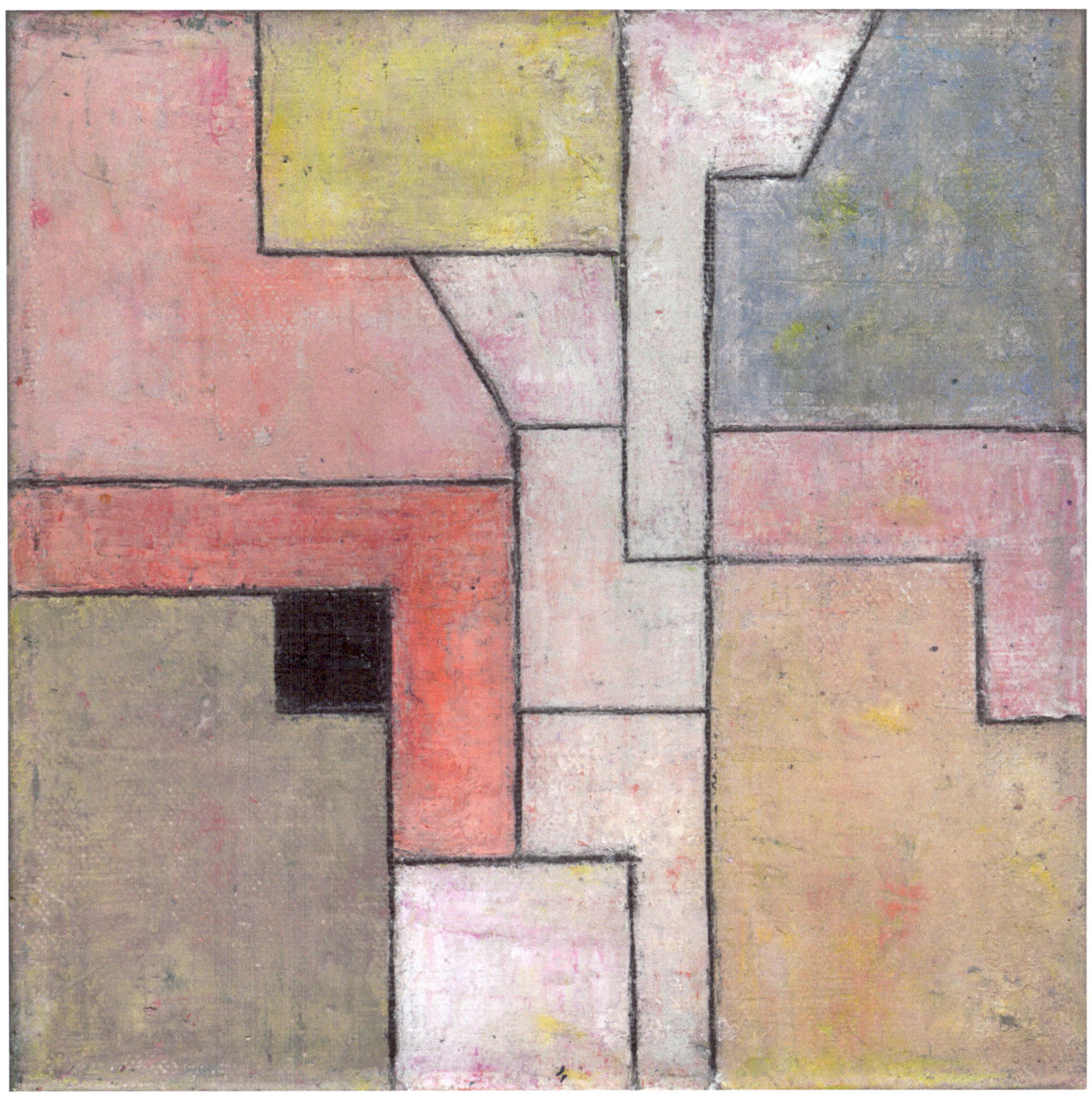

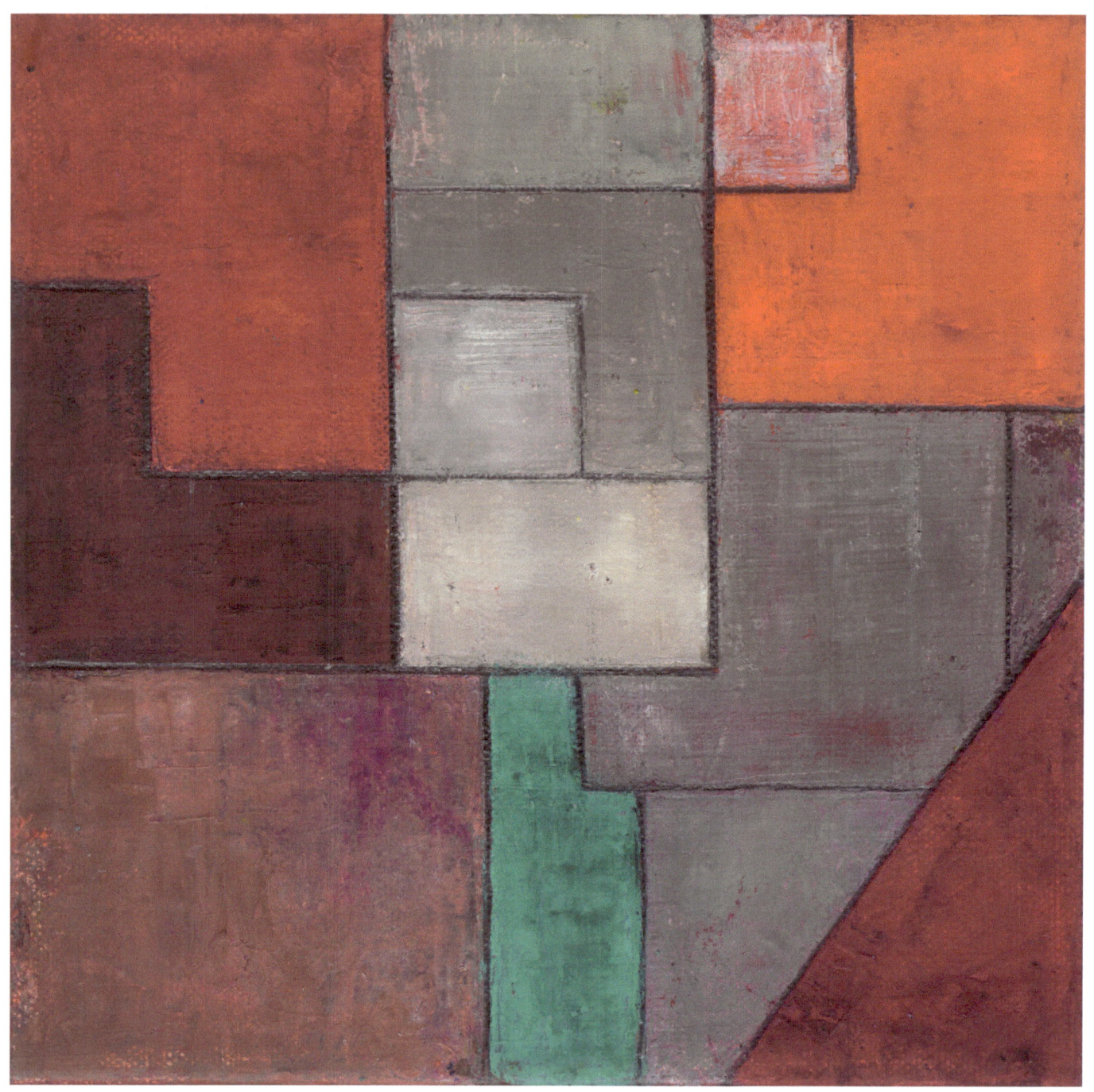

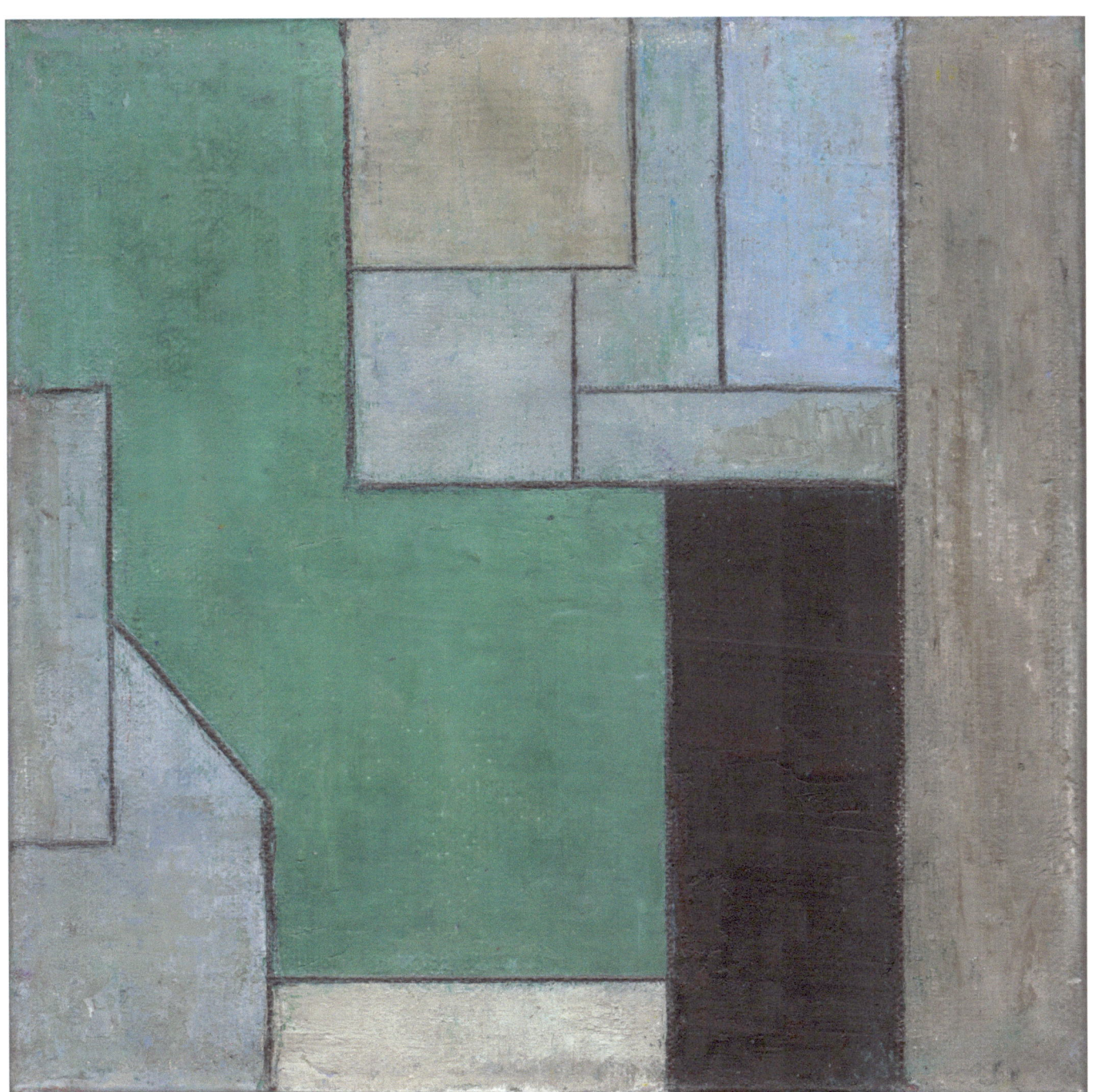

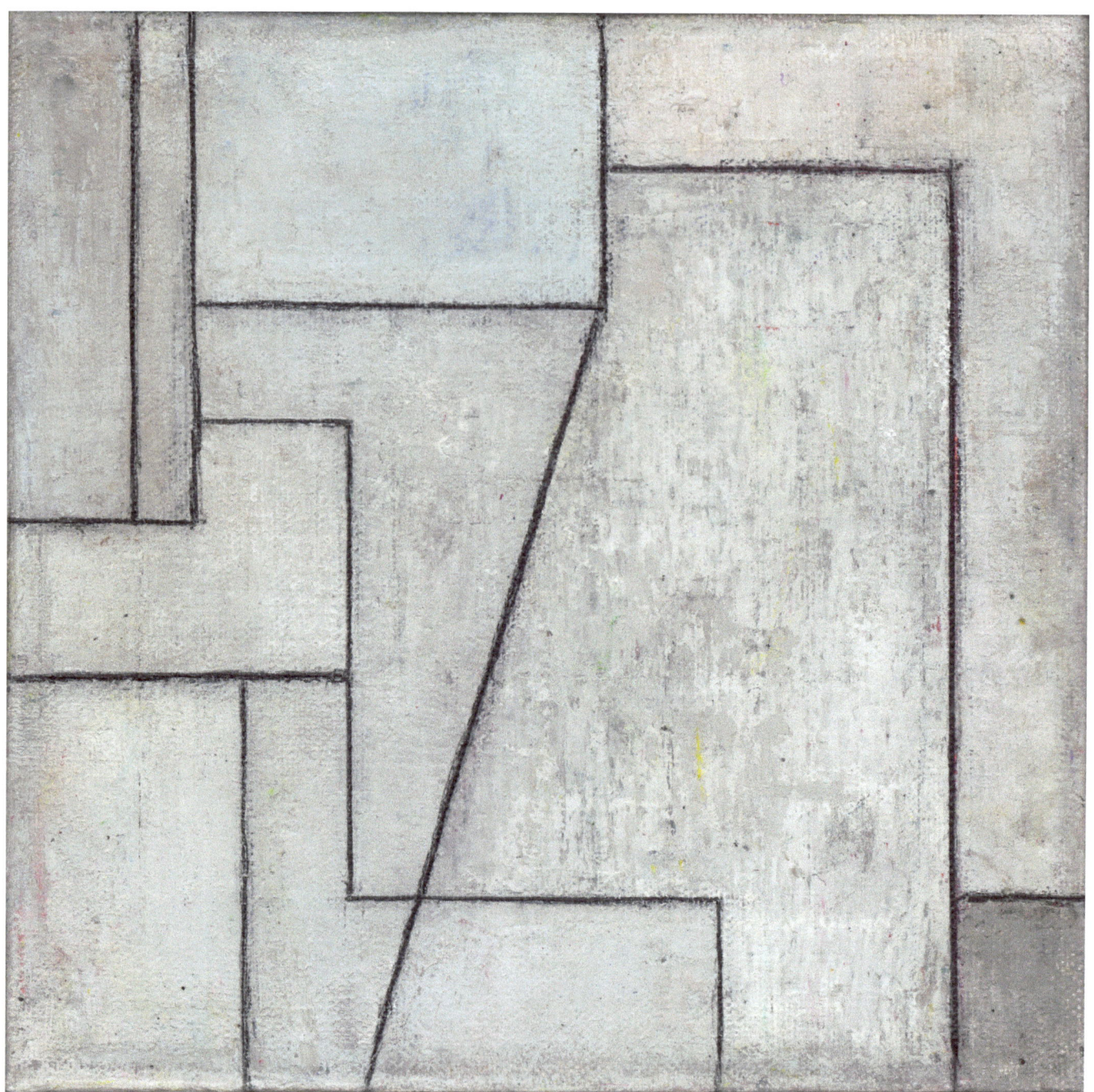

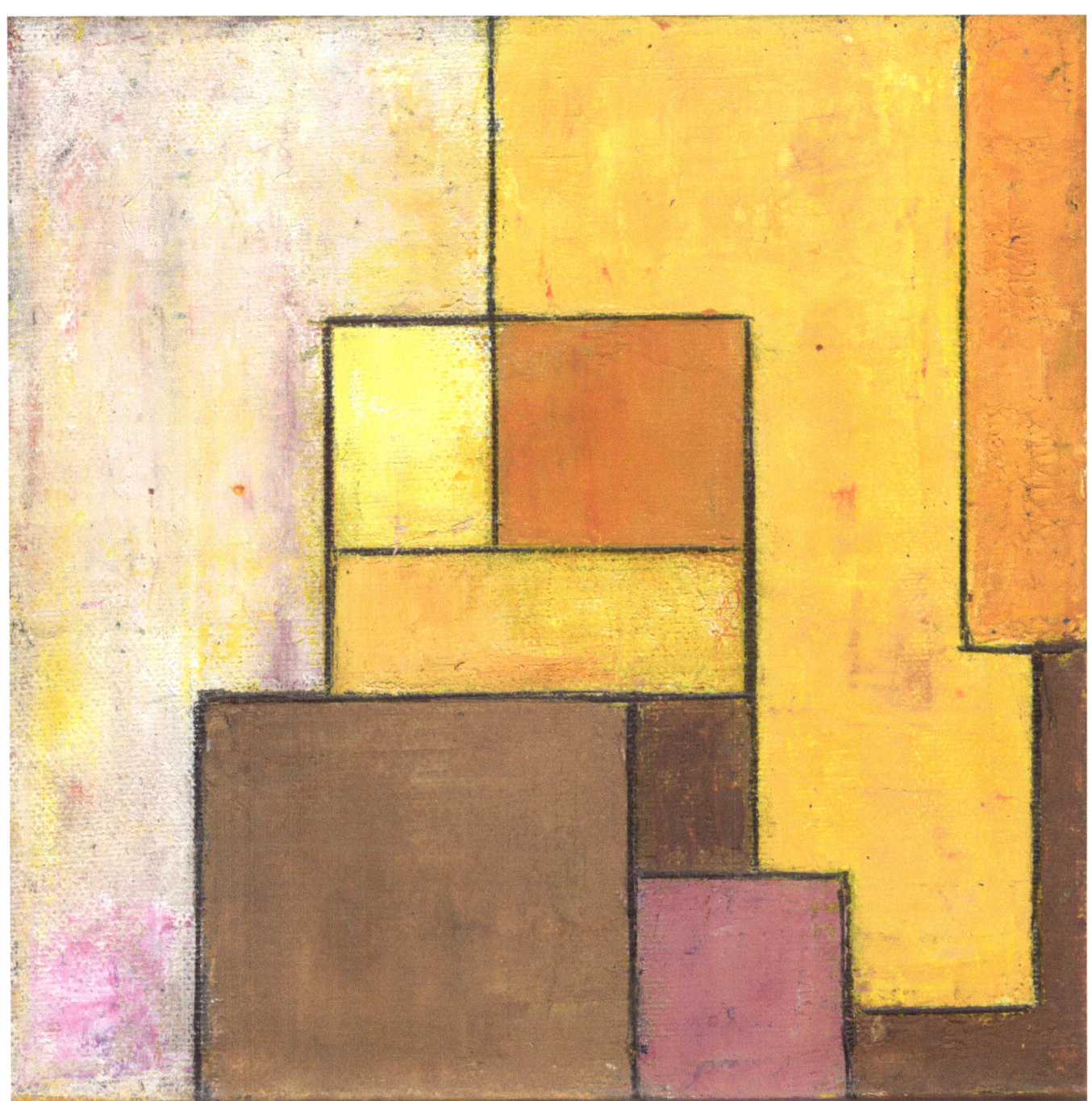

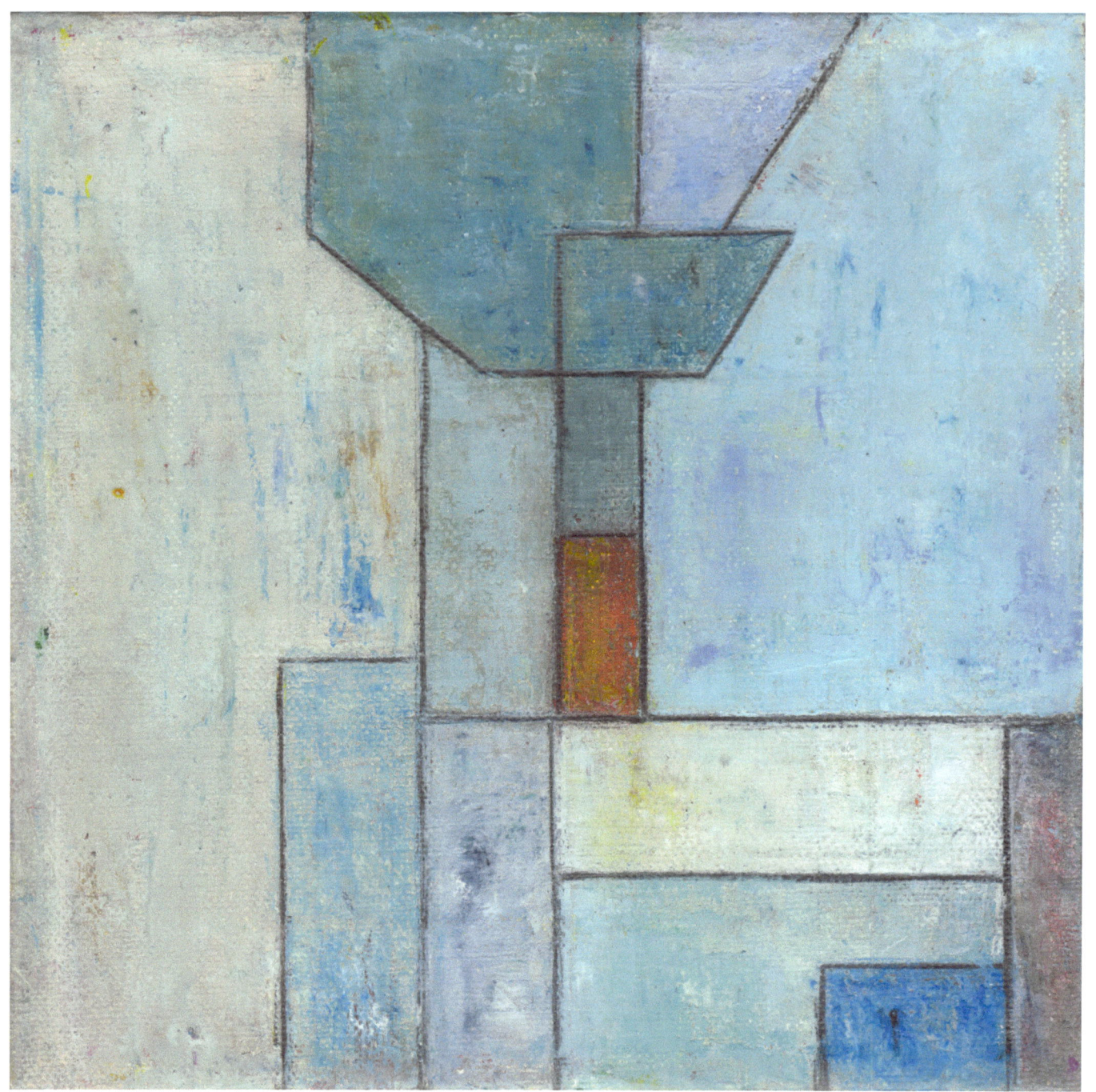

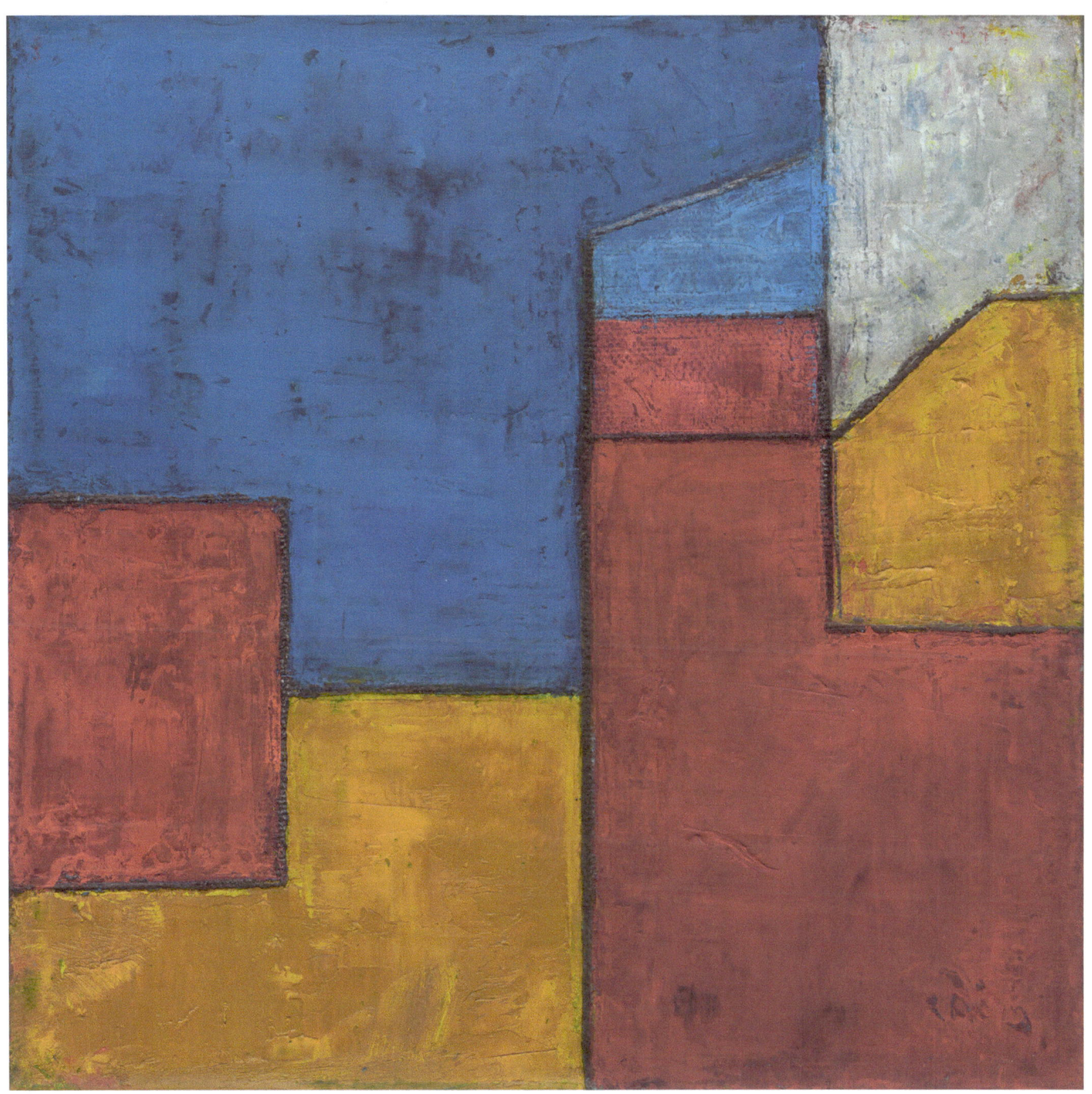

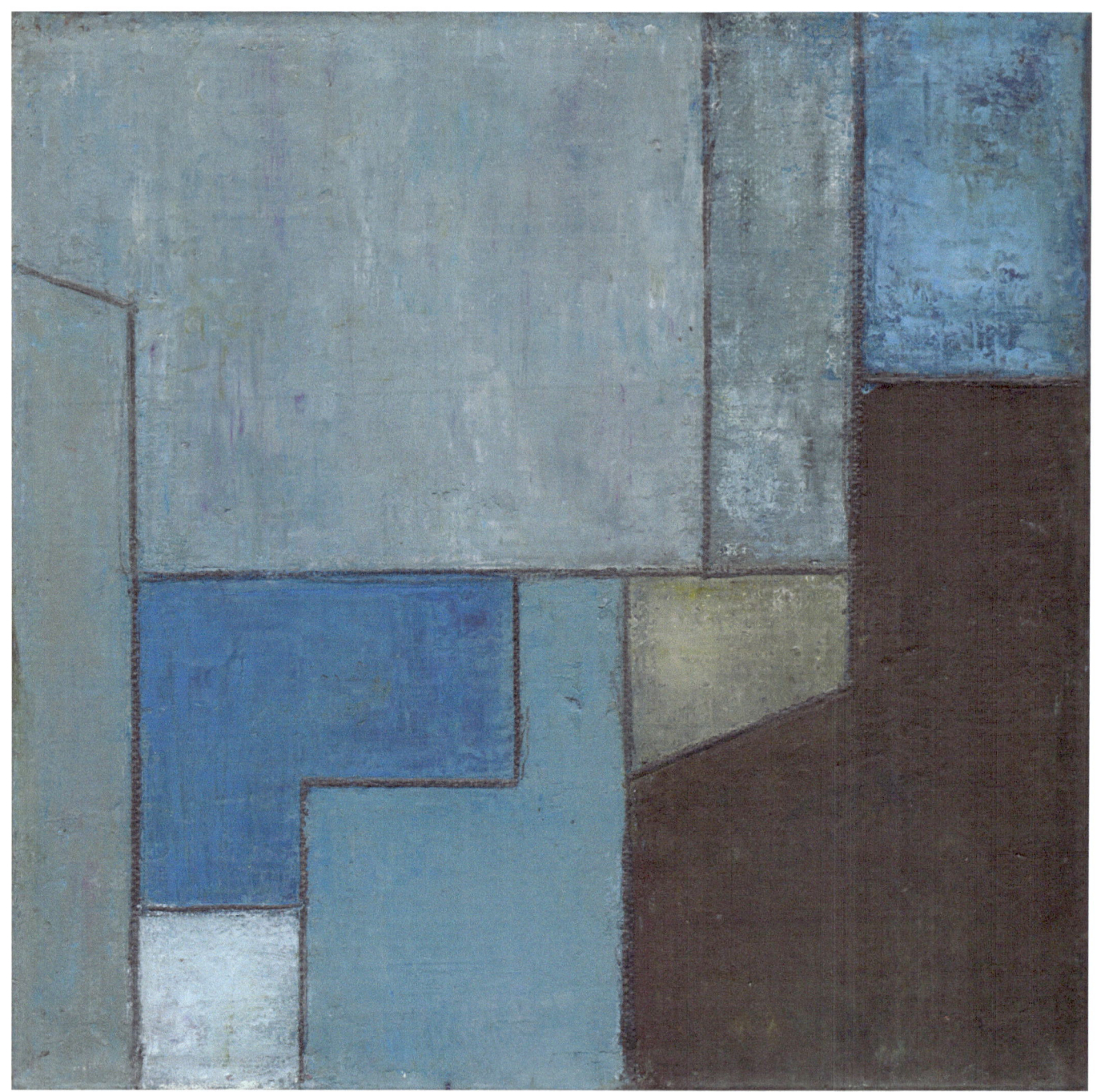

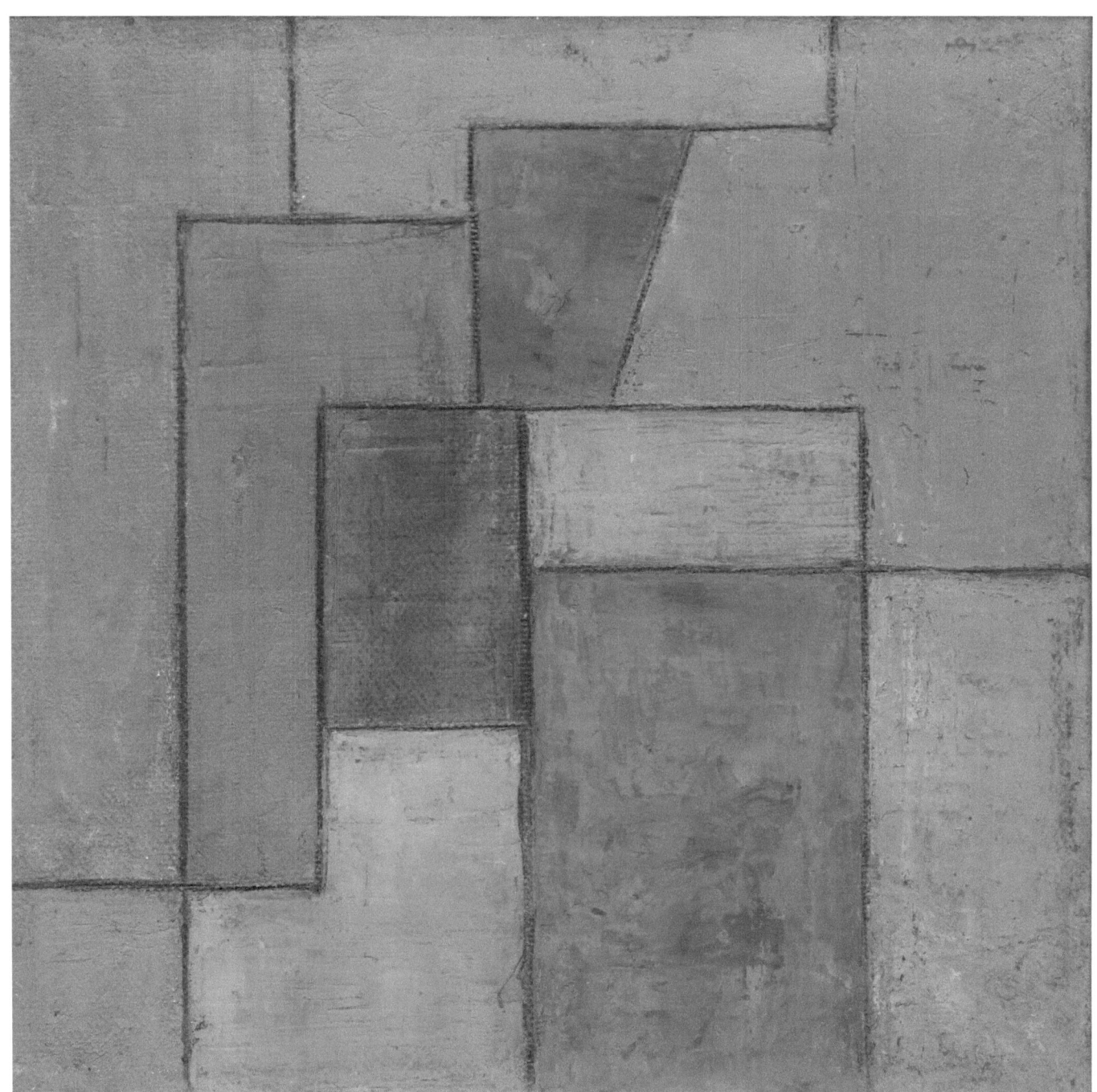

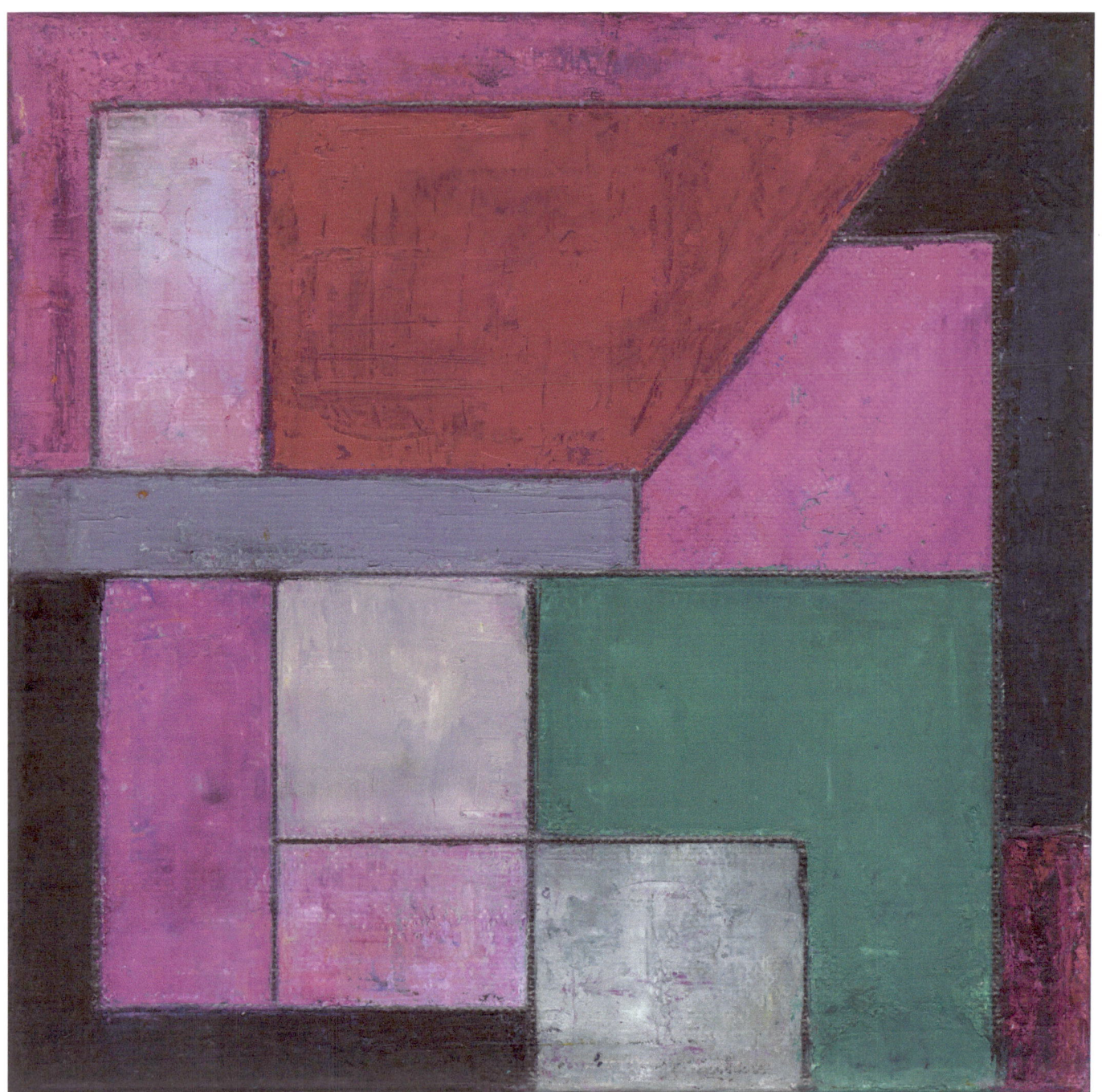

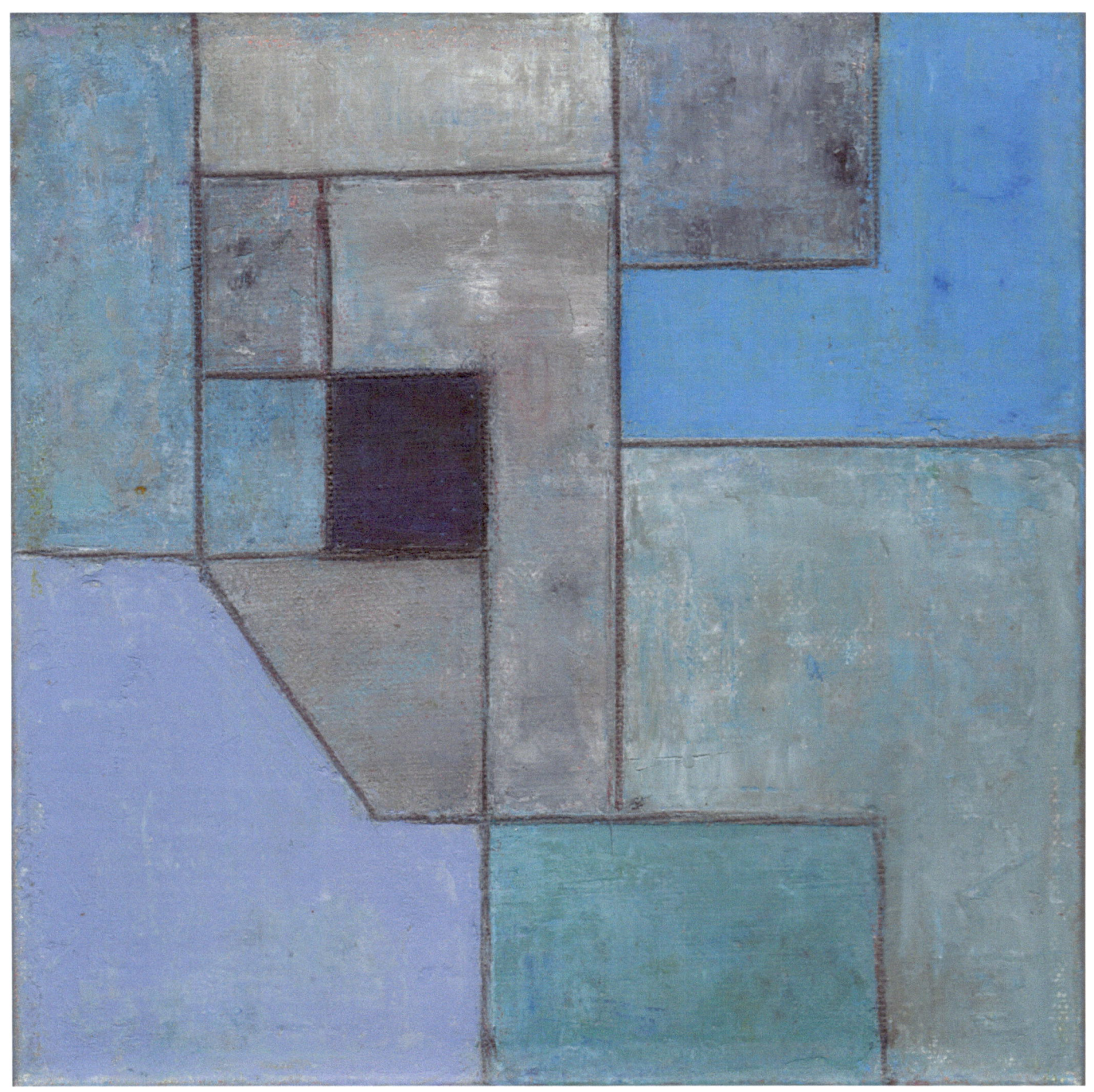

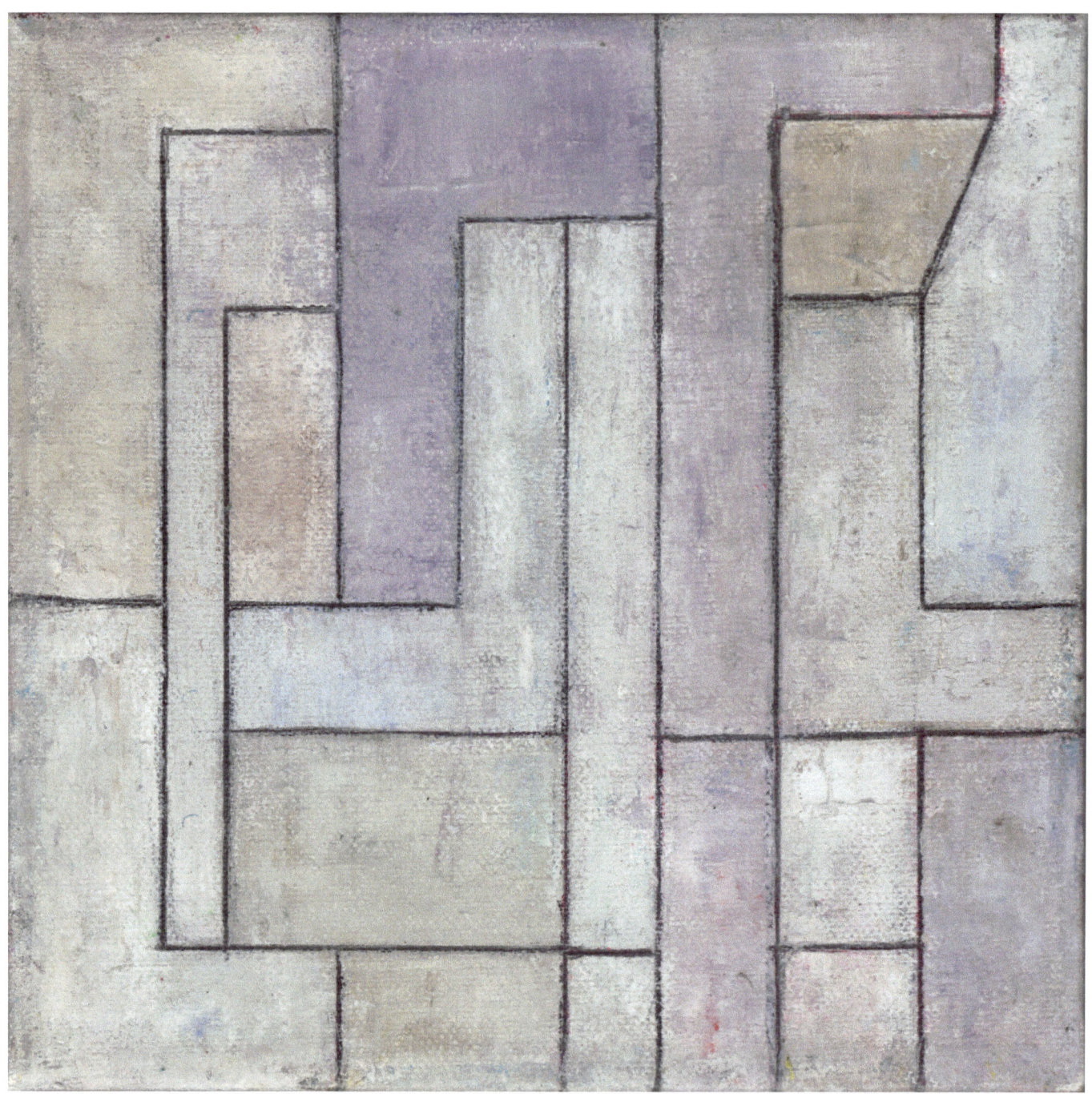

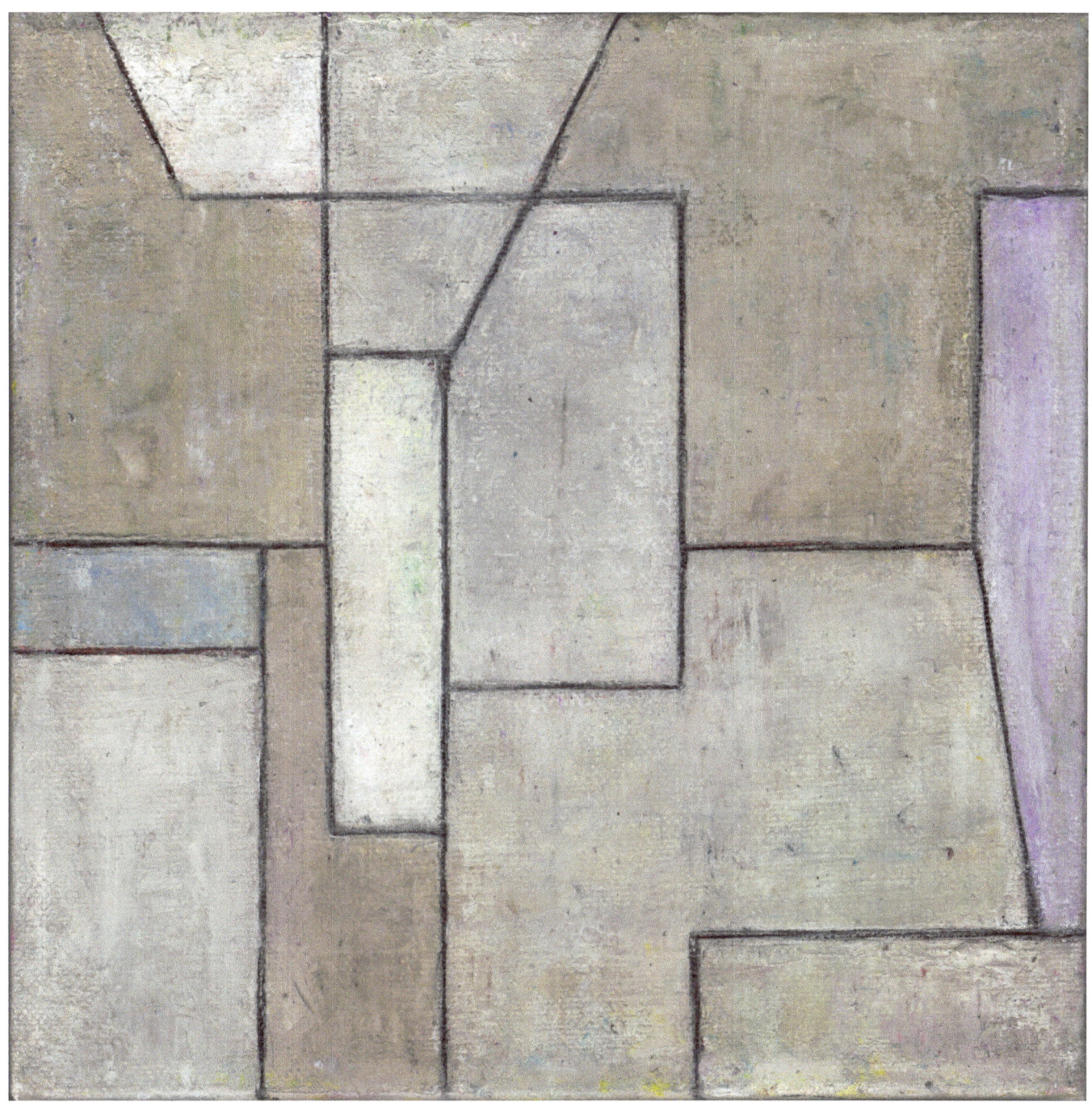

21

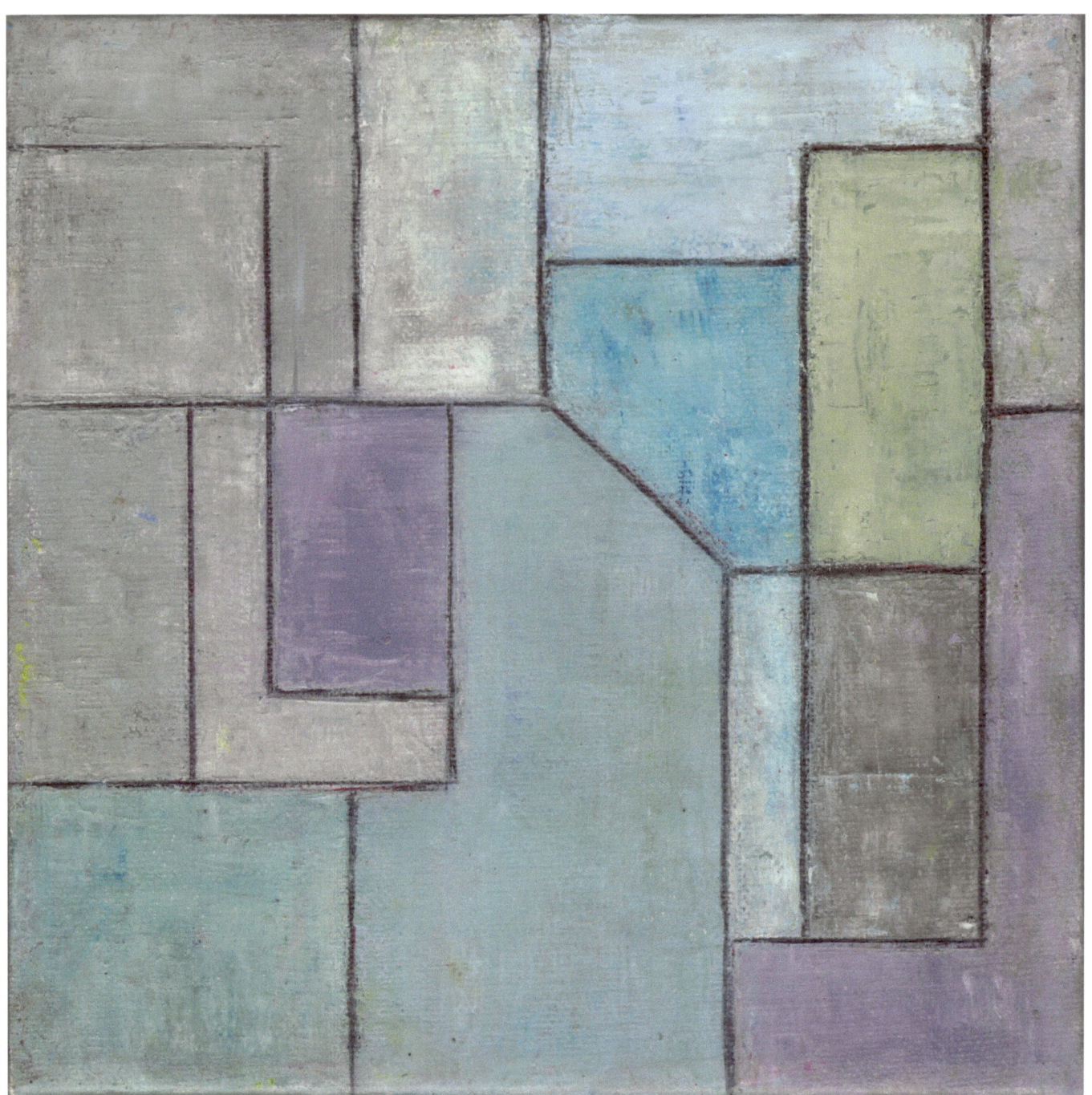

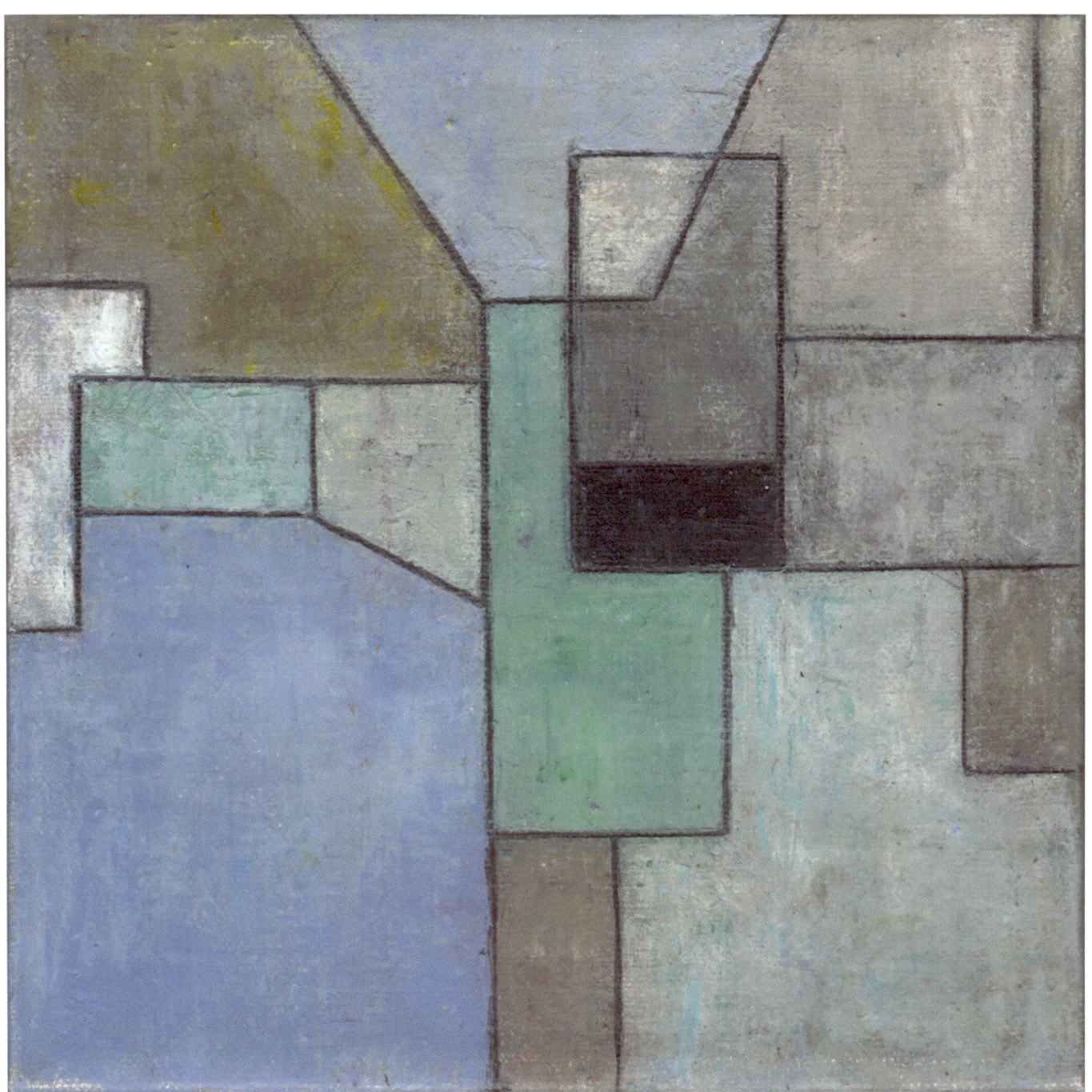

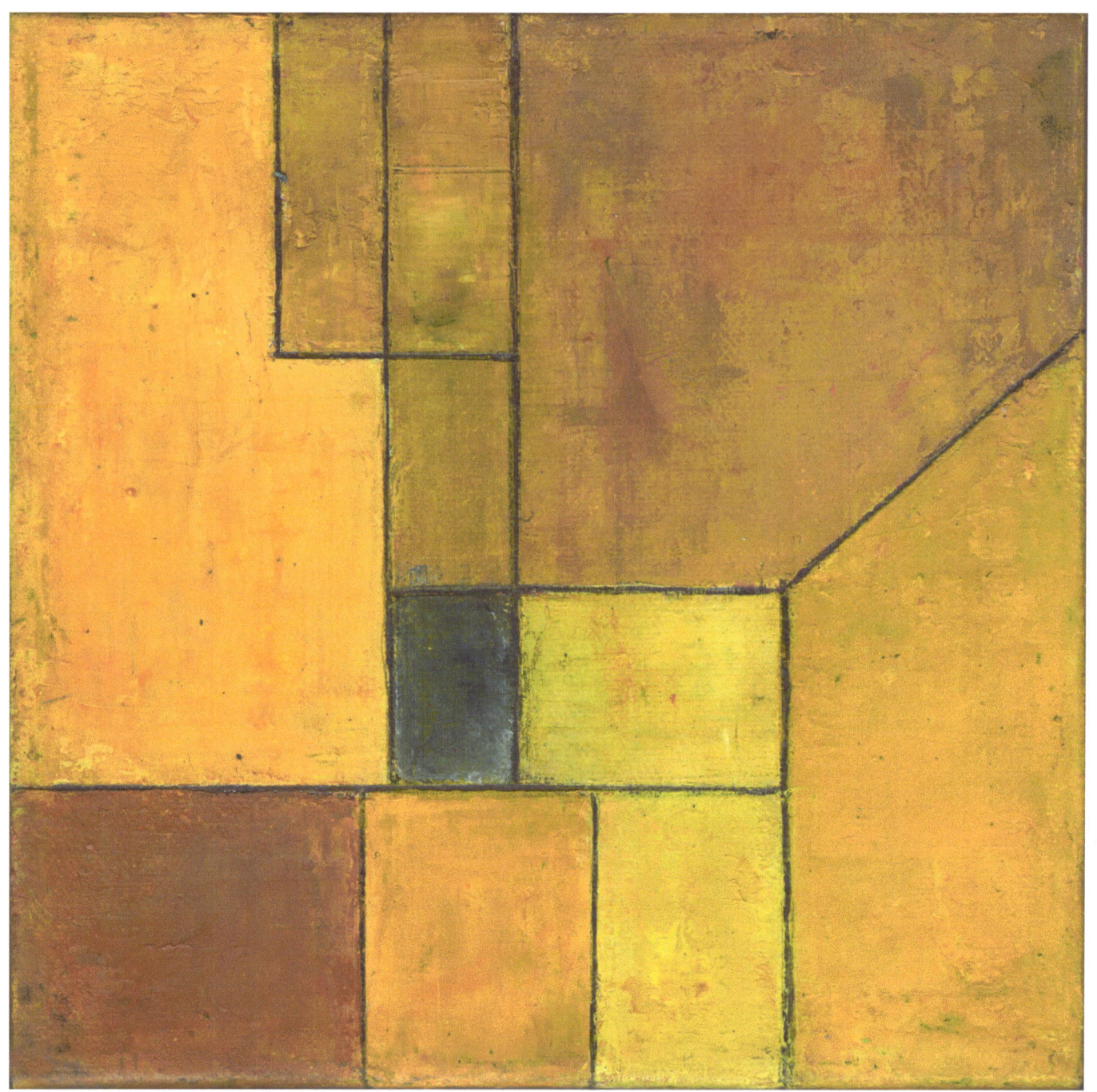

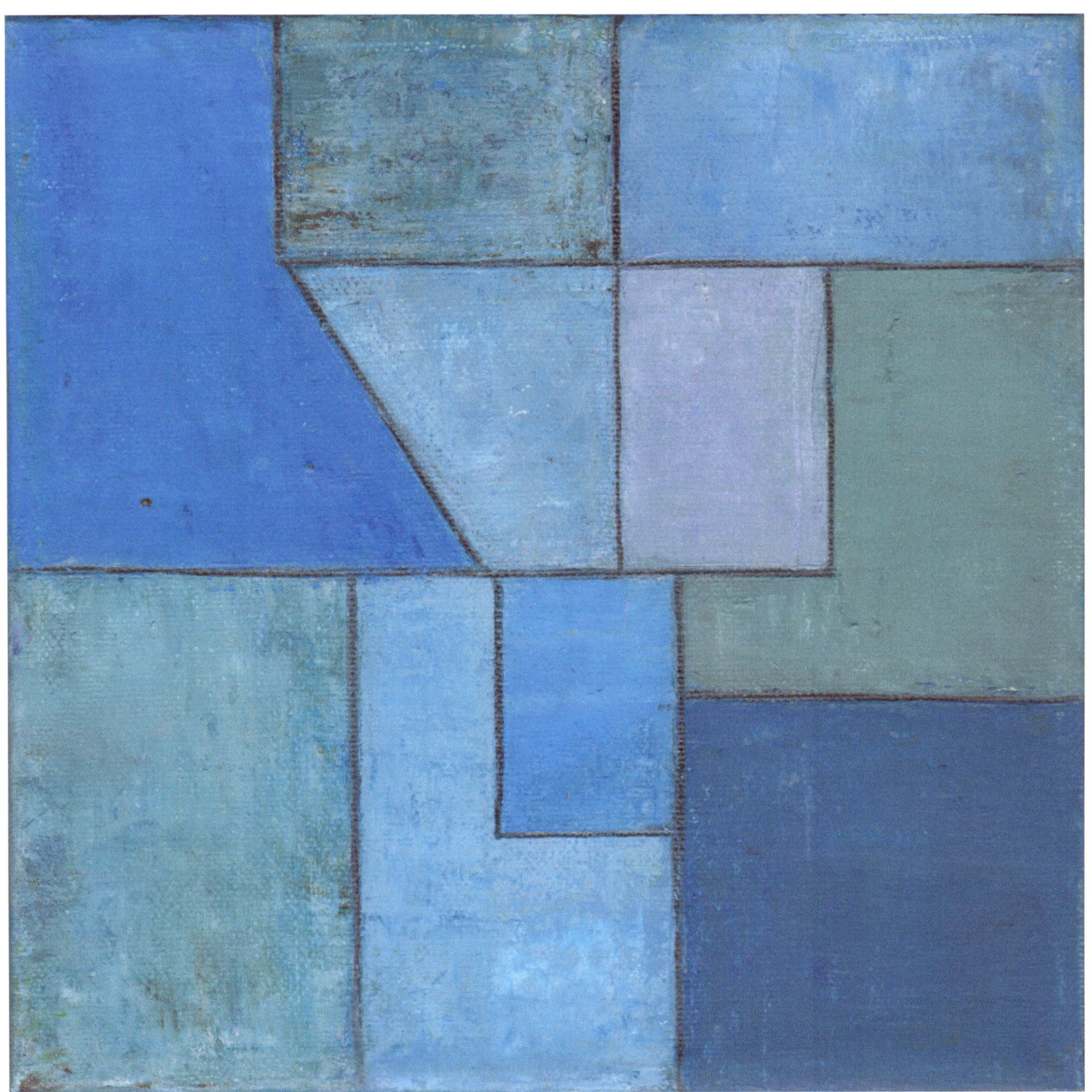

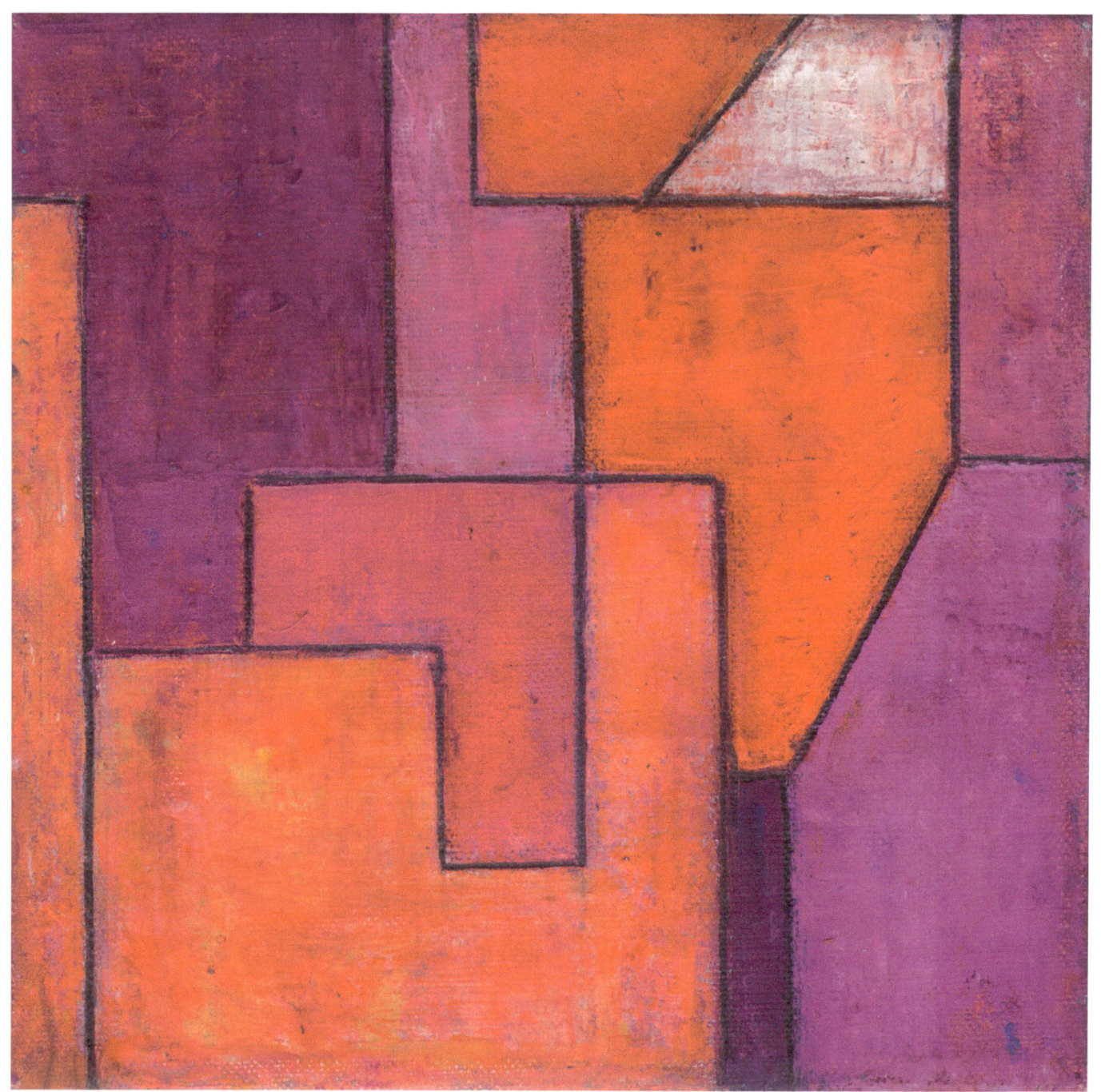

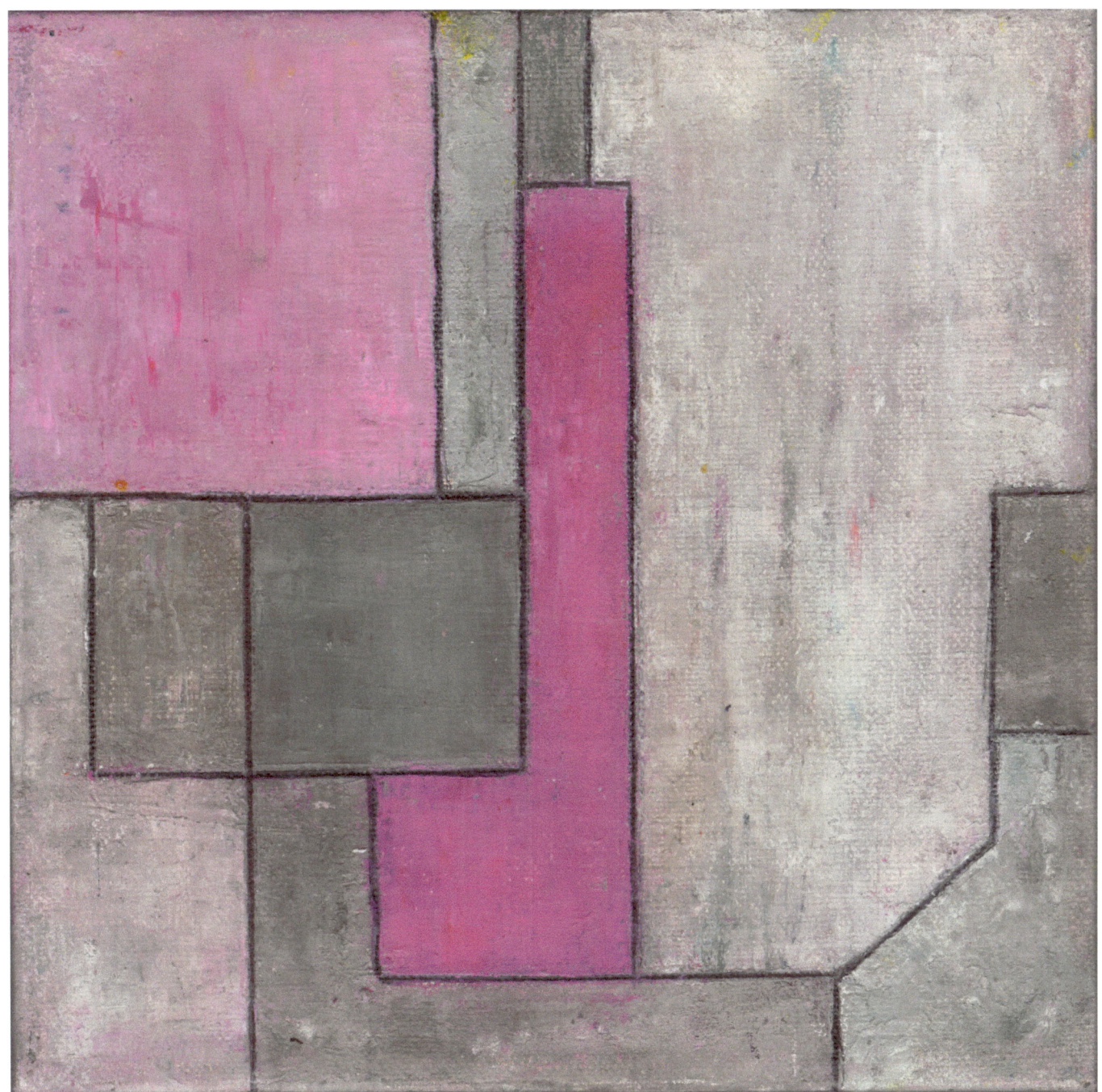

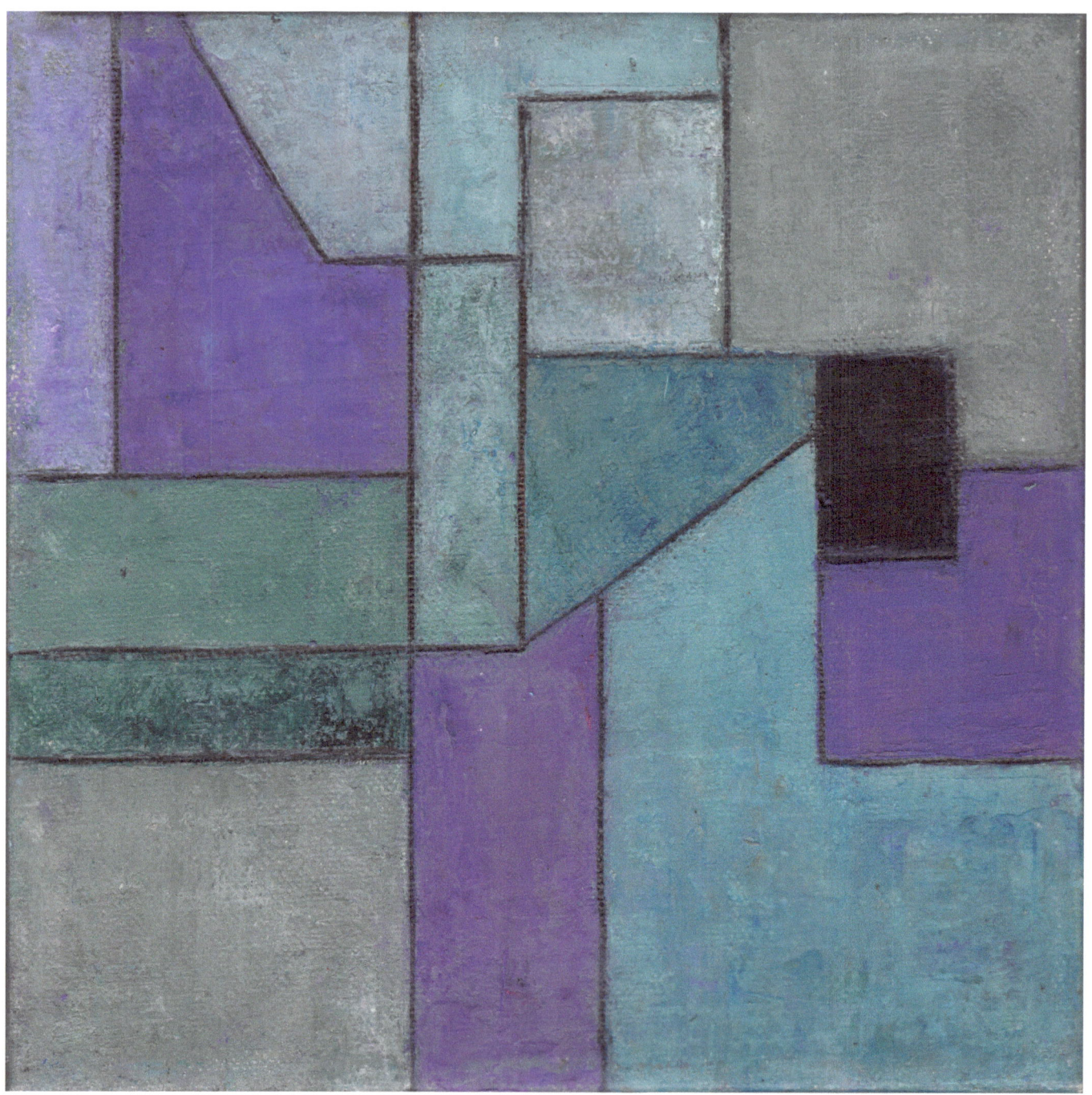

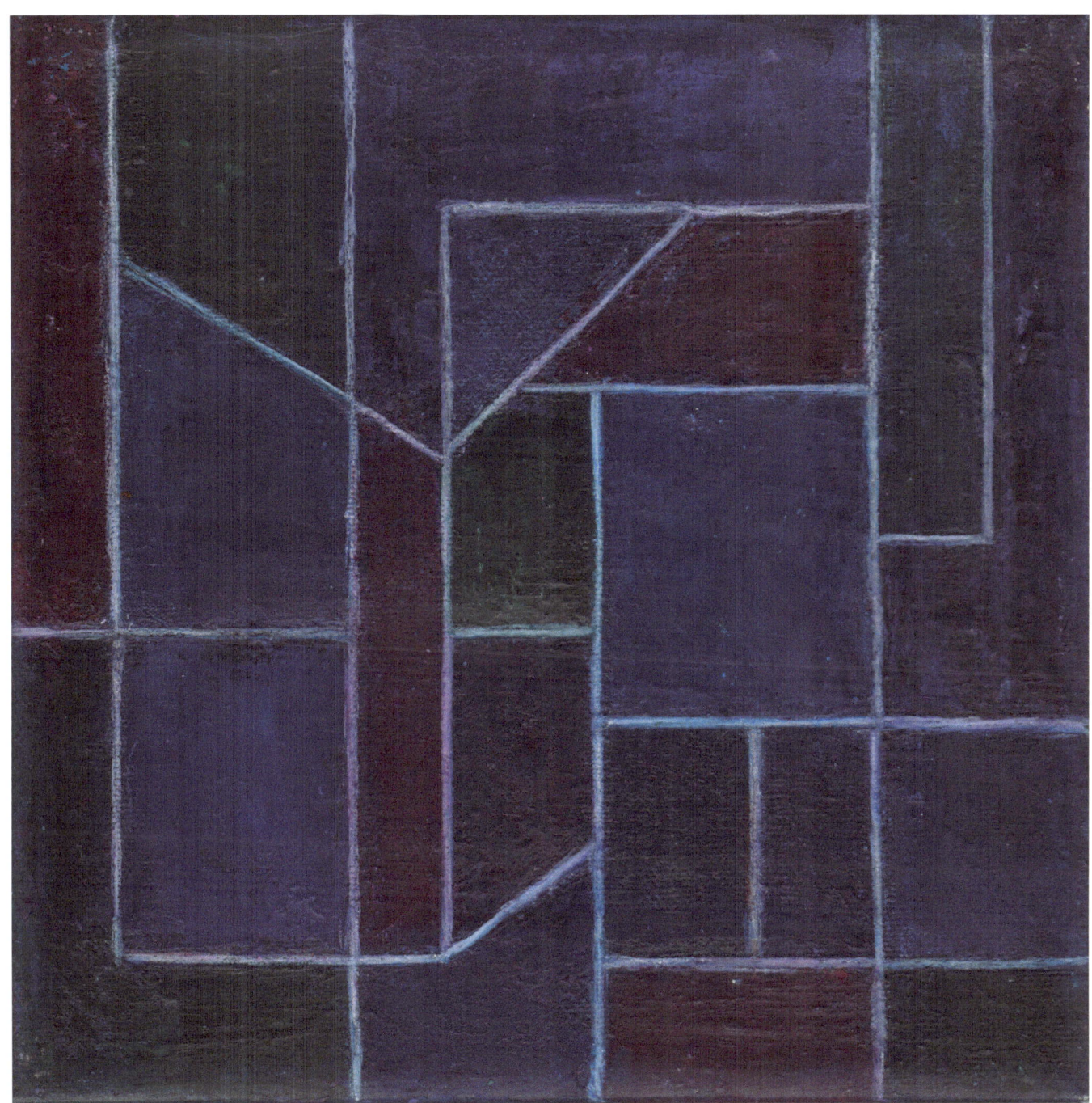

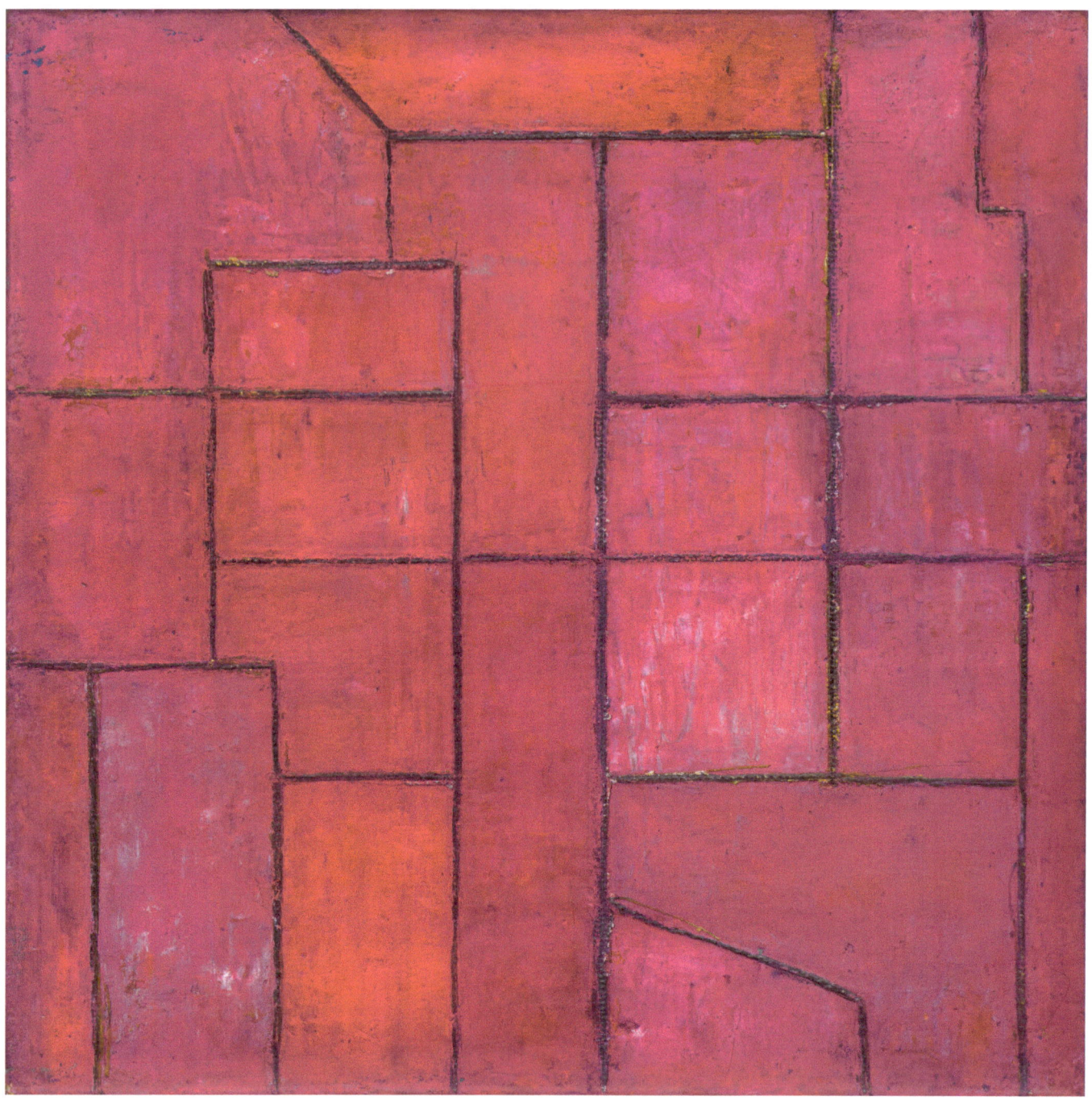

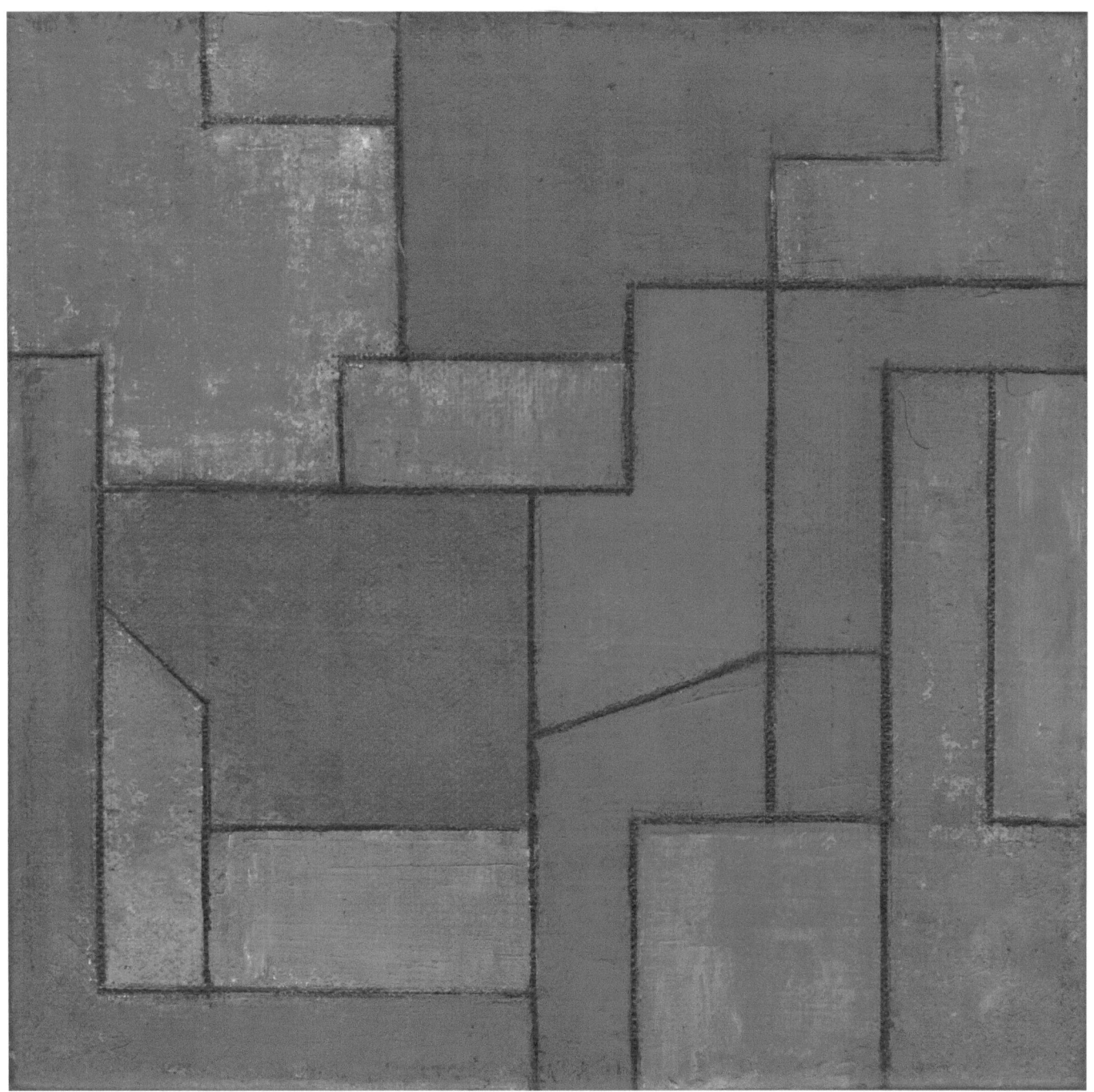

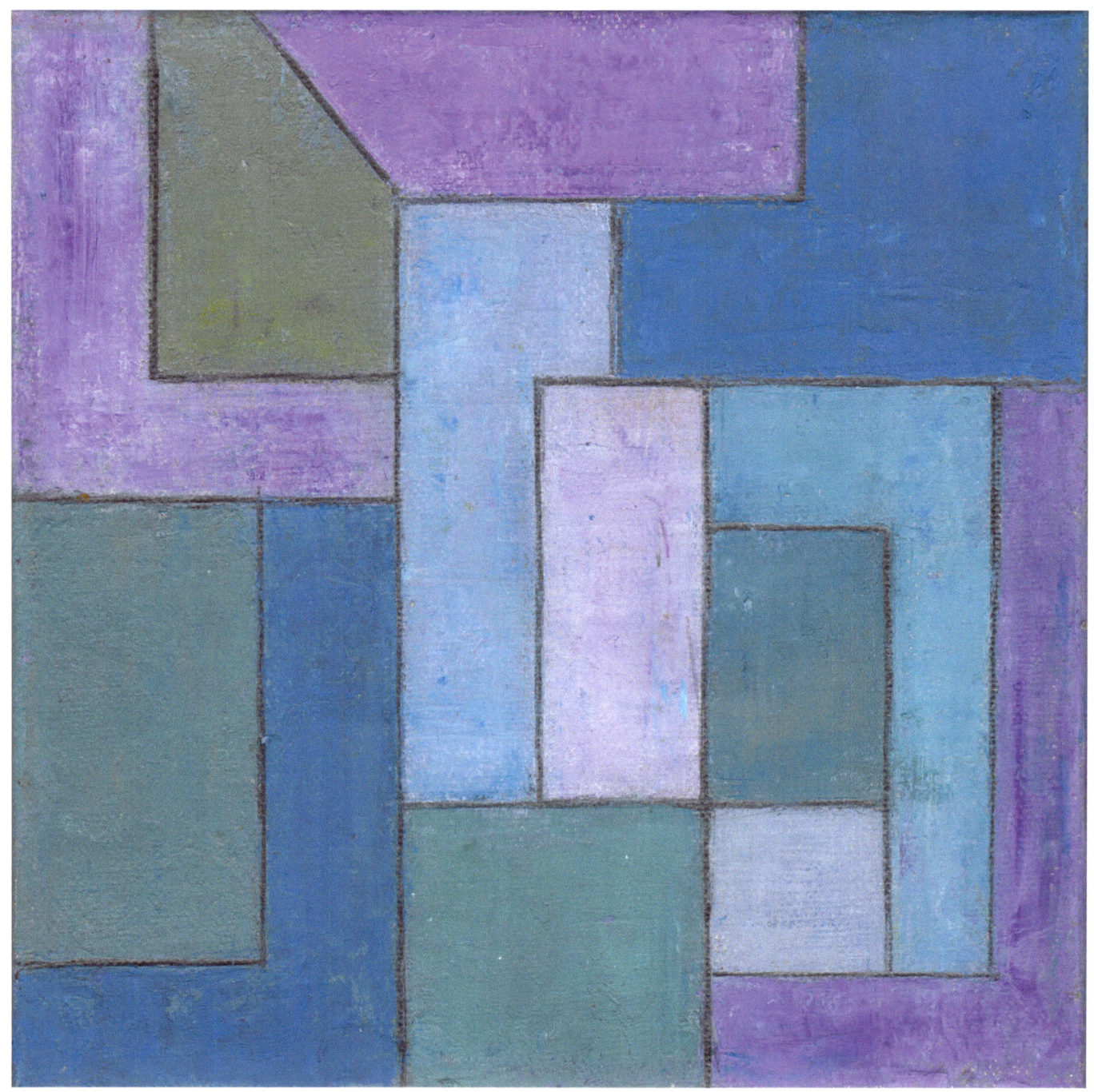